PHILIPPE KAIZEN

I0421249

LIE DETECTION SECRETS

Detect and counter-attack a person who tries to lie to you in just a few hours of reading !

PHILIPPE KAIZEN

LIE DETECTION SECRETS

How to detect lies and improve your watchfulness

Philippe Kaizen

Dedicated to all my family and all my friends and to you !

I am grateful to you for buying my book.

With respect and the best regards,

Philippe Kaizen

THE SUMMARY

What this book will bring to you

The aim of this book is to teach you techniques, which will enable you to detect the lies among your interlocutors.

You will develop a greater vigilance and will be able to detect and counter-attack a person who tries to lie to you.

No need to learn by heart all gestures, techniques or reflexes, you have just to understand the functioning of psychological and physics reactions that occurs among liars.

Around this basic mechanics, we will study together some frightening techniques which used only or associated will help you to face peacefully difficult situations.

Welcome in the small book of lies detection, I wish you a good reading!

Chapter 1

INTRODUCTION

Do you have a job interview in few days? Do you want to buy a basic computer but you are submerged by information that the salesman gives you because he hopes to sell the more expensive model whereas a less powerful model would make the deal very well. You want to buy a second-hand car and the man who affirms you that this car is in very good state but you don't know anything in mechanics and you want to know if he is honest?

Do you suspect your wife having an adventure and you want to know the truth discreetly? Does your child hid you his new passion for the cigarette or his bad marks and you need to know all about his new habits?

What about to have a new habit like detecting the lies? You don't need a special machine. Just to know one or two theories about the functioning of the reflexes add to some tricks and you'll become a lies living detector!

When we lie our body reacts, these reactions are almost uncontrollable.

This little book of lies detection is organized in the following way:

Chapter two, is about to know where these famous reflexes come and why it is very difficult to control them, you will understand in a simplified way the brain functioning.

All techniques you will learn in this book are based on the reflex mechanism so you will be able to easily distinguish an honest reaction of a built reaction.

Doctor Roger Sperry is known for his Nobel Prize of medicine about his works and discoveries on the two hemispheres of the brain.

In chapter 3, I will speak about these discoveries to understand the functioning of the brain and especially to discover the relation between the lies and the orientation of the glance when your interlocutor lies.

Indeed, you will be able, after reading this chapter, to know if your interlocutor calls upon his memory or if he makes up the words.

In chapter 4, you will immerse yourselves in the concepts of spaces and geography; it is not a subject about physics or geography but rather about space occupied by a liar. We'll look at his behaviour, his gestures which will betray him.
These techniques result from my different experiences; as a poker player and in my job during witnesses' examination or questioning when I was a police officer.

Chapter 5 treats of logic and the common sense that you will be confronted with verbal reactions can have people who hiding truth or lying.

In chapter 6, you will approach the various strategies to detect the lies as direct attack or technique that consists in detecting signals without to attract attention. In this chapter, you can be sure of that, you will go onto the attack.

In chapter 7, you will find some additional keys and advanced techniques of lies, used by the liars and being the result of my own researches.

At last, **the final chapter** will deal with:
First, my method of mental coaching which is about self-control (how to stay clear-sighted when you try to detect lie in a difficult situation).

And second, the techniques that will enable you much to assimilate more quickly any information or competence (you will become a live skilled detector of lies!).

What a program!

Before beginning the theory, I would like to catch your attention about important points.

- First point, to detect the lies requires training and rigour. However, don't be afraid, this training is very simple and any one can do it and become an effective lies living detector with regular practice.
- Second point, it's very important to make difference between the fact to catch a sign of lie and to call your partner a liar.
When I see signals of lies, I create in my mind a small list of reactions that I located, and at the best moment, I confront my interlocutor (for example a salesman who wants "to swindle me"). Last point, in this book I will use "she or he" to nominate a person who lies without particular preference.

OK, now let us start our small trip in the brain.

Chapter 2

THE LIES AND YOUR BRAIN

To understand the basic mechanism that makes possible to detect the lies, let's go to make a small trip within the brain. Don't worry, you don't need to be a neurologist and there are no complex theories, only simple and clear explanations.

This chapter is very important because when you will understand brain functioning and after reading this book, you will be able to detect when words don't reflect real thoughts without storing all liar's movements.

The goal of this book is to give tools that help you in any situation.

I'm sure that you have already been surprised by an event which suddenly faced you and you have been so surprised that you were overwhelmed by emotion.

Typically, emotion makes you react in different ways; it freezes you or it helps you to take flight. Your reaction is just a consequence; you have to focus on the emotion itself and its origin which are the key point of the lies detection mechanism.

This reaction is extremely fast, instantaneous and it is practically impossible to control it. Why practically? Because with practice it is possible to reduce these reactions to a certain extent, for example the most experienced professional players of poker learned how to control themselves to generate the least possible of gestures or reflexes which could translate the value of the charts in one way or another that they have in hand. In fact the people who have a bond with a field where it is necessary to have a great self-control to face difficult situations or stressing can have a certain predisposition to control it. But have no fear, on the one hand the percentage of people having a great self-control is weak and on the other hand with this book you will learn how to detect gestures, words, reactions even with those who control herself with the offensive techniques that we will see in the following chapters. And finally, for those which want to learn how to develop, amongst other things, certain self-control, the final chapter is entirely dedicated to them.

When we are in this state of surprise, when for example a person asks us a question which we did not expect at all, our body reacts instantaneously, by movements. They can be a movement of head, eyes, eyebrows, mouth, arms, feet, bust, in short from any parts of the body (finally almost). It is immediate, and it is thus very difficult to hide them. Then, when we decided to lie we are under a certain emotional state (a state of stress) which could be turn into others gestures or movements which will betray us in full view of someone who can detect the lies. The lies will be detected, and it is also a very important point in detection, by the words. Not in any tonality or speed of flow of the words but in the logic of the answers themselves.

To be brief, it does not matter the level of self-control of the interlocutor, his lies will be revealed in one way or another, instantaneously or in the end.

The common denominator to these reactions reflexes are the emotions. And these emotions are generated in a quite precise place of our brain, the limbic system!

The brain can be broken up into three principal parts, like you can see in the following diagram:

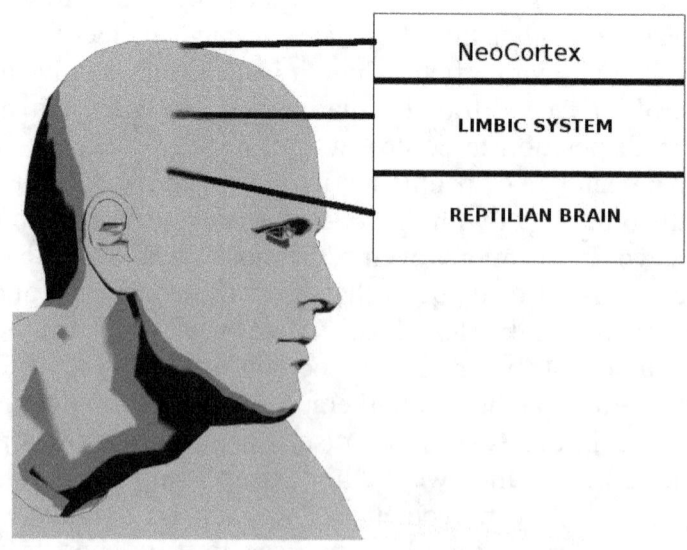

We can represent the brain in the shape of three layers; major names the brain reptilian which you can also find under the name of R-complex system. The layer of the medium places what one calls the limbic system and the higher part of the brain names the cortex or neocortex.

The major part, the reptilian brain, has the role of controlling all that is automatic in the process of operation of our body. For example it is this part of the brain which controls our breathing, the temperature of our body, manages the blood pressure, controls our rate of heartbeat, all the operation of the vital elements of our body. It is also the center of the vital needs such as the sleep, the reproduction and food.

The reptilian brain would be, on all the evolution of the human brain, the oldest part but the most vital part!

However, it is not this unit which will interest us more.

The parts which will interest us are the limbic system and the neocortex.

The transition course named limbic system, is the part of the brain which is the base of the comprehension of the mechanics of the lies detection.

Why?

Because it is here that the emotions and the memory sit. In fact this system is much more complex than the simple fact of dividing it into two elements, in fact it is a whole of structures dedicated each one to precise spots, but the two structures which are the emotions and the memory will be those on which I will concentrate.

The limbic system exerts a control on the nervous system, some glands (like adrenalin for example) and takes part in the system of survival of the human being. But above all it is in this part of the brain that the emotions are managed.

When we are surprised by an unspecified event which emerges in front of us it is our limbic system which immediately, takes the control of the situation and to this event, an ultra reflex makes you react. When we say that your emotion took the top, that your blood made only one turn, it is fault of this limbic system because it generates itself these famous emotions that you could not control in the last difficult situation with which you were confronted.

The limbic system is also closely related to the process of memorizing, in fact, it was even established that memorizing is an emotional process. As you can note it, the emotions have a really great role in our life and not only in the detection of the lies!
When the effect of "surprised" was managed by the limbic system, information passed to the part of the brain called neocortex. The neocortex is the part of our brain which has the biggest size. One can define this element of the brain as being the seat of the thought, of the conscious thought. This neocortex thus receives information from the limbic system and then we try consciously to manage this situation, while trying to calm us, while trying to take again our spirits and then to make an adequate decision (or not). It is not rare for example in even professional players of poker, to detect a limbic reaction (it is under this term that I will define now these reactions) where the player will be surprised (brilliant! I have a pair of ace), will immediately position his hands in a position of confidence then after the neocortex, the conscious thought, will tell him "attention! you are posting confidence, changes the position quickly! ", the player immediately rectifying the position of his hands giving to his adversaries an opposite impression (which it has in fact in his hands the weak charts).

The neocortex is divided into two hemispheres, often named left brain and right brain, each one having quite precise specificities which we will approach in the next chapter on the relationship to the movement of the glance. Indeed according to the direction which our glance at the time of a reflexion takes, we call upon our memory or we create, invent something.

The two elements of the brain of which it is thus important to include/understand operation are thus the limbic system and the neocortex.

You understand now the operation of the limbic system which is instantaneous, which reacts by means of emotions and which thus makes react the body by various channels.

Why is this so important to understand the limbic system?

For the two following reasons:

First point, you can consider the following rule right now: since the limbic reaction is instantaneous, controllable with much difficulty, that it comes from the emotions managed by the limbic system, it is thus **sincere, spontaneous, and if it is sincere then it is not invented of any part by the "conscious" brain**. We can establish the opposite of this rule, if a reaction is not spontaneous, immediate, then it has all the chances to be created. When you offer a gift to a person, if he has a reaction of surprise or an immediate joy, it is that he had a limbic reaction, therefore sincere because he appreciated your gift. If he expresses joy (by simulating the surprise) for more than one second you will have understood that his conscious thought took over and thus this vain joy is a "creation". However, if he does not like the gift either, you will certainly see a limbic reaction which will be expressed by quite precise gestures that we will have all the time to explore in the next chapters.

Second point, and will have understood it to you, to detect the lies, it will be enough for you to surprise your interlocutor and thus to make enter in action his limbic system which will make him react in the form of gestures, movements, then of words which you will not miss, I am certain, to intercept!

A direct question with your interlocutor concerning a significant subject will make his limbic system react especially if you put initially this person in a state of confidence. With the advantages and disadvantages which comprises a direct "attack" of course.

And if you have miss this limbic reaction ? or if your interlocutor could control his reaction and that you are not sure on what you saw?

No problems! Once you question your interlocutor, he will be in a state of stress, which is a strong emotion and despite everything the efforts that the liar will try to carry out to hide this stress, his emotion will always end up being translated into gestures reflexes (stress is equal to emotion and thus equal to limbic system).

We will also see in the next chapters that it is not inevitably necessary to attack someone directly, you will be able to make react his limbic system without his knowing and thus obtain information !

To conclude this chapter, all the foundations of the detection of the lies is located in the reactions reflexes of the limbic system, honest, sincere, instantaneous, that it will be necessary for you to start with your interlocutor by several methods, direct or indirect which we will develop together in the next chapters.

But since we are always in the meanders of the brain, let us carry on with the study of the neocortex and its two hemispheres. Also important chapter because it will bring the concepts necessary to you to know all the secrecies of the orientation of the glance. You ask question to your interlocutor, and then he try to answer by directing his glance towards the line. What does he think about? Is he calling upon he memory or is he inventing a history?

Welcome in.....

Chapter 3

THE LIES AND YOUR EYES

As you noticed, when we reflect our eyes go from one side to the other one. Is there a link between this fact and true or lies? I am sure that you have already heard in some Police serials a performer claimed, "He lied! His eyes looked in this side". Ok, what is your opinion about that? Do you think it is real or just a joke?

It's definitely true, I can assert you that there is a link between both events, depending on what we say we don't look in the same direction. Moreover, it is beyond our will, just a conditioned reflex.
Is this a limbic reflex? Not it is rather a reflex of limbic post-reaction.
For example if you ask your friend about Where he was last night between eight and ten you will surely witness a limbic reaction and then, according to his innocence or not, he will start to think about the question that you asked him.

To think about something, it is either to call up our memory, or think up a tale.

Our brain is divided into two hemispheres, each one have precise functionalities and according to our need (call up memories or invention), our glance will be directed in a specific direction.
It is very difficult to control this movement and even if we could it, it will betray us just a split second.
After reading this book, you will be able to see this fleeting moment.

To understand our fantastic brain functioning let's go spending some hours together. My research about this subject was inspired by Doctor Roger Sperry works, the Nobel medicine
Prize for his works about the brain functioning and his discovery of the two hemispheres and their distinct functioning. Dr. Sperry's work focused on patients whose their Corpus Callosum, had been cut after surgical operation in order to treat epilepsy. The only way was apparently to cut this part of their brain system better known as a set of nerves, which connect the left, and the right

brain. After this operation the two hemispheres were no longer connected.

Dr. Sperry then made some experiments, which allowed him to discover that the two hemispheres function in different ways, the left-brain controlled the right side of the body and the right brain the left side.

The subjects must fix the center of a spot on a screen. On the left of the screen appeared the KEY word; on the right the word APPLE. As the optic nerves are connected to the hemisphere of the opposed brain, the left-brain perceived the word APPLE and the right one the KEY word.

When the patients said what they saw on the screen they stated to have seen the word APPLE but not the KEY word.

After this experience, Dr. Sperry noted a different functioning between the left and the right brain hemisphere. The left one was able to describe what it saw; Dr. Sperry deduced a sequential and logic functioning (in this case one letter after the other).

Their right hemisphere recorded the KEY word, but it is not able to describe it. He deduced that it surely be a holistic (a global) simultaneous, conceptual, metaphorical functioning, in short the opposite of logic.

In front of the patients various objects were stored of which an apple and a key. When he asked patient to take with his left hand the object that he had described (the apple) patient took the key! (His left hand being controlled by the right brain and having recorded the key).

According to Doctor Sperry research, the left brain is the place of logic, analysis, creativity and its functioning is sequential (i.e. one thing after the other). Therefore, we use the left hemisphere when we want to analyze, create or invent something.

The right hemisphere intervenes in conceptual, holistic or intuitive thoughts (understand the opposite of logic). When we call up our memories, we use the right hemisphere.

We can declare that the left hemisphere is those that we use when we lie, invent and the right one to say the truth. When we call up our memories, we look for something true, something that we have already lived or experienced.

Now it remains for us to establish the link between the two hemispheres and the glance orientation. Look the following drawing to understand what is about :

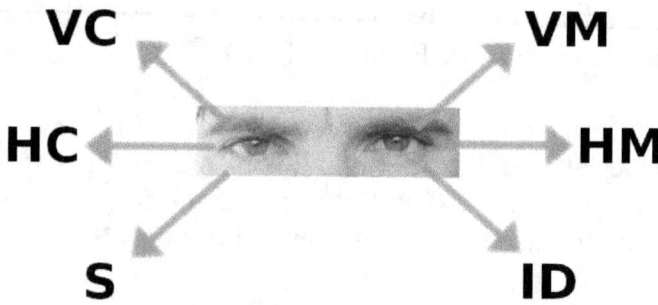

Here are the different ways towards which your glance can be directed when you reflect. To be clear, imagine this drawing as if you had this person in front of you, when I say that he calls up his memory or that he invents something, he will direct his glance to his right-hand side or left one.

If you prefer to imagine the scenes compared to your glance, you have to reverse what I will say.

Let us imagine, dear reader, that we have this person in front of us. I ask him some questions:

Do you remember your first car color ? Then his glance will be directed in way V.M (V.M for Visual Memory), in top and towards his left.

We know now that the right hemispheres is the one which call up our memory, and as the right hemispheres controls the left part of our body, we will naturally direct our glance to the left!

Could you imagine a pink cow? As he have never seen a pink cow, he will invent it and need his left hemisphere to do that, his analytical, creative brain will help him to represent this pink cow. Of course, his glance will be directed in V.C (VC for visual creation) his right hand and to the top.

Do you remember the voice of your grandmother? ». As he calls up his memory, his right hemisphere starting to work and his glance will be directed to his left, but more to an horizontal way (H.M direction, on the drawing, means Hearing Memory).

Could you imagine the sound produce by the village church tower, if the bells were in your living room? His glance should be directed towards his right and a more horizontal line. In fact, we urged him to direct his glance to a H.C (H.C for Hearing Creation) way.
Richard Bandler and John Grinder works in N.L.P (Neuro-Linguistic Programming) revealed two types of glance directions, which are I.D and S.
ID (Inner Dialog), as if the fact to talk to ourselves helps us to think.
The S as sensorial implied when we call up to memories with body feelings, as when you answer to this question: "do you remember the lake where we had a bathe this summer, and how the water was cold?

Now, you have a new technique of lies detection, when your interlocutor look towards his right hand, you will be sure that he will give you an invented answer. Conversely, when he turns his glance towards his left, he deals with his memories, you can consider that he says the truth.

According to my practical background experiences, I focus my attention on this fact : if someone call up his visual or hearing memories or not, and corroborate it with his eyes direction. Now the trick is to do the same thing.

To go into detail, left-handed people would tend to reverse what we have just seen, the call to their memory would be made with right direction. Why, it is very difficult to know it considering the multiple studies and contradictions about the subject.

Don't worry this detail concerned only the eyes glances, you can also ask your interlocutor an innocuous question which will call upon his memory and you will see his glance direction.

All the techniques, all the reflexes, movements, gestures, which you will see in the following chapters, will be the same for anyone!

Ok, now let us go to study three examples:

First case, in the evening your boyfriend returns later from his office because from time to time, he used to take a glass with his colleagues, and you know that sometimes his colleague, Miss X, took part in it.

You cannot help thinking that your boy friend finds her more sympathetic than he says and you would like to know if she is often present.

You ask him if miss X was present this evening, he answers that she was not with them, so you going on with another question, "how long have you crossed her in the bar ».

If he directs his glance towards his left-hand, he calls up his memories and tries to remember the last time he saw her in the bar. If he looks to his right side, he's going to create a tale and you can be sure that either Miss X spent more evenings with them than he told you or she was there tonight. Maybe he lay to you but it could be possible that he doesn't want to worry you and invents this story.

You have to examine each situation, let us not rush to conclusions. On the other hand, his glance direction is the sign that he invented his answer; you can carefully register this clue on your mental list in the lies column.

To know the real story you have to carry on the research and it is precisely the subject of the following chapters.

Second case, you have a child who goes to school; you know that it is time for him to bring you his report card to make you sign it. However, sometimes it's happened that his report, by magic, never arrives. Do not spoil your effect, ask your child about where his staff meeting should take place.

If your child starts to look toward his right-hand, then you can sure, that he creates the date he will give you. If he tells you that, he doesn't know when it will take place and looks towards his right he lies too. He knows very well when the staff meeting will take place.

Nevertheless, if he looks towards his left, he calls upon his memory and he will tell you the truth.

Third case let us take again the case number one with your boy friend but in this case, he had already learned and memorized an answer to be ready to answer your question.

You understand that now things will be a little different.

You ask him whether miss X was present this evening, he answers you she was not with them, then to look a bit more closely you ask him: "how long have you crossed her in the bar ».

He could for example answer you "Oh, it's about two months that I did not see her" if he directs his glance towards his left, he says the truth because he calls upon his memory.

When you will read this book and will practice my techniques, you will add to the orientation of the glance many other techniques that will make you understand that something is wrong with the glance. You will be able to understand when the answer is created or learned to mislead you.

Don't worry, you will see, in the following chapters and especially in the "logic and the good direction" chapter that depending on the words used, or sentences are constructed, you can find clues which will enable you to know if someone lies or not.

Moreover in the strategies chapter you will learn how "to tackle" these ready-made sentences. The liar, not having been able to prepare all the possible answers, you will have to
tackle some points of the answer you'll press him to call upon his creative brain to invent news of them and of course directs his glance towards his right-hand!

You have now with an effective technique to determine if your interlocutor invents or calls upon his memory when he will going to give you his answer. Do not forget that one day you
can meet a left-handed person and that will reverse glance orientation. Think also that your liar, sorry, your interlocutor could learned his answer.

Now, we will shift into high gear speed with the following chapter…

Chapter 4

LIES AND BEHAVIOUR

Now, we are going to study behaviors, gestural and postures of the body we have when we lie. The most important thing of this chapter and even of the entire book is that you will not have to learn thousand postures and gestures to detect lies.

Four precise points must be understand and take in. If you understand these four points functioning, then you will be able to detect a liar by his body behaviors. That will help you to tell truth in from falsehood in difficult case.

Don't worry, that presents no problem, you just need to read what follows!

According to the situation in which we are (without speaking about lies), we have different body behavior. According to our mood or physical feelings, we will have different bearing.

If you have dinner in good company, you agree that you will have a different attitude than if you were with your boss or even your mother!

Do you have the same behavior when you take bus or when you are quietly walking in forest?
We act differently when we are in restaurant or in employment office.

I hope it…

However, let's get back to the subject, the liars? Well it is the same thing, someone who lies will have the same, positions, gestures and the funny part of the story is that you will be able to provoke them…

Let us study now the four key points, which are the most important of this book:

1. The limbic brain

2. The space concepts

3. Self-massages

4. Words and reflection of the thought

In chapter one, we dealt with the limbic brain, now we are going to link it to the reactions and the gestures that fellow on from this. The limbic system has a link with the space concepts and self-massages about which I will speak later.

When you ask a question that surprises your interlocutor, his limbic system reacts, you know now that it is a fast and spontaneous reaction.

For example, you were invited to the restaurant by one of your colleague and as you are not indifferent to him, you accepted it. In the restaurant, you discuss one thing and another, even about couple relationship. You drawn to him and you consider love affair with him so, you want to know more about his opinion about couple relationship. To create an effect of surprise, win his trust (you will learn how to do in the next chapters).

By the way, let's suppose that he's already in this state of mind. Therefore, to know his innermost feelings, you ask him: "I am a serious and faithful person, and you? At this moment, your interlocutor is surprised and his limbic brain reacts.
Body movements, more exactly space movements, which are always in three directions, express the reactions.

1.Escape

2.Body freeze

3.Aggressiveness

Either he will have a gesture of retreat, or he will freeze or become aggressive.
What is the difference between the three reactions? No one, these are different space directions, but mean the same thing: your interlocutor feels ill at ease with the subject.

He can react in various ways: escape: "this question makes me uncomfortable, because I am not always faithful, I must flee! ». If he moved back and leaned on the chair for example, it is a way to say "I'll move away to hear no more about this subject".

He can be rooted to the spot, as a prey, which freezes hoping do not to be picked out by a predator. On the other hand, he can attack or be aggressive in order to frighten you and make you change subject.

If your interlocutor is at ease with this subject, he will not suddenly have space movements, and you can consider him as a faithful person or an honest one who will confess his infidelities.

The analogy with the prey and the predator is perfectly exact; it is the way that the animals react to a predator when they feel in danger. Our limbic system is in close connection with our survival system and proceeds in the same way. If you cross a street and a car which you did not see came charging straight at you, you will have a space limbic reaction: escape (to dodge the car), or you will freeze. It seems difficult but you could also attack the car.

A space limbic reaction is the first movement that you must identify when you want to detect the lies. It is the sign of his implication in the subject, even that he feels in danger.

These movements are in general short, as all the body moves you can easily see it. It can be a shoulders and head faint, but if it is linked to your question, it's a limbic reaction that started. Freezing is rather a short reaction for a liar to recover his mind and just after he sends out other signals that you will learn later recognize.

Those body movements are generally followed by others gestures like arms gesture for example, but the most important thing for you is to understand this first and second point.

After this limbic reaction, your escort will pass to post-limbic reaction. Let's start with the assumption that he has something to reproach with.

Let us study the action in slow motion!

This post-limbic state is a state of stress, because your interlocutor has to answer this question and does not think to escape by the nearest exit.

Stress implies emotion and emotion is linked with the limbic system, which is distinguished by the reactions. As the interlocutor must answer the question, several things could happen in a short time, like protective gestures towards the one who generated this stress.

We will study in details traditional gestures of protection with some pictures. Don't forget that he will have theses specific eyes directions, already study in the last chapter.
He has to think about an answer and now, you know, according glance direction if someone calls his memories or creates a story (a lie).

This post-limbic state can also precede an appointment with someone. If you know before going to an appointment that you have to tackle an important subject, you
will not be very at ease. This stress will make you generate

reactions during the dinner (as long as you will not have tackled and settled this subject).

In fact, where there is emotion there is reaction. In the restaurant example, Mister X is stressed because the woman inside him wants to tackle an important subject. At this moment, he starts to self-massage (third key point). We can find this act in many gestural reactions and if you understood that, you do not need to learn all the gestures, because self-massages are the most recurrent.

If you are in restaurant and you cannot evade the question, you will surely be stressed.

What will you do to feel better? You will try to relax! To relax, in those situations we have the same gesture, which is...

To massage a part of our body.

Do you want some examples? Ok, When you put your hand to your brow and rub it with your inch and your index or when you touch your nose, in fact you make, without realizing, a face massage (outside the fact to scratch your nose).

When you rub your chin with your inch and index (there is no mistake, you do not scratch it you rub it), it is the same thing when you massage your forearm, lips or cheeks. Your hands on your thighs you make backwards and forwards movements, you rub them, exactly as the massage of a muscle, with your hand, your inch, your fingers, you pass and press more or less hard on the muscle to slacken it.

If you massage a part of your body, it is because you are in an emotional state of stress, and you are stressed because you are implied or you feel ill at ease with the topic of conversation.

There is another gesture which is little more subtle, his hand over his mouth, his inch on one side of his lips and his index on the other (like someone deeps in his though). If the inch and the index are fixed then this person is think, if his inch and index make a small massage (from lips to the cheeks) he is stressed and tries discreetly to calm down. I noticed that many times when I play poker, or even chess. Yes, we can guess that something just happened in the head of your opponent even when you play chess!

Like everybody else, we have this reaction to massage ourselves, I still repeat it, it is a needless work to learn by heart all positions, you will often found this reaction and you have just to notice it to understand what occurs in your interlocutor head.

Let's get back to the subject, what Mister X will answer? "Yes, I am faithful," if he says that rubbing his ear lobe, you know now that when he rubs his ear lobe he tries to cool down because of your question.

Would Mister X feel in danger? Is he ill at ease with the subject that you have just broach? Most probably!

Let us go on and start the fourth and the last point (the link between words and thought). As Mister X answered the question, we can compare his response in his state of stress. Mister X claims that he is faithful, however he is stressed and you note it because when he answered, he shrank back and he rubbed his ear.

You can establish the following fact: the words of Mister X are not in agreement with what he really thinks. Therefore, in this precise case, you just detect that he does not think what he has just said, HE LIED (you can put it on your mental list concerning this Mister). You will see in the next chapter, according the answer that Mister X can give you; it is also possible to detect lies.

Personally (although in the case of the restaurant it is rather obvious), I prefer to note that his words are not in accordance with his thought rather than to call him directly a liar.

There are many possible situations and it is better to cumulate different signs of lies before confronting (or to avoid) this person. You can ask with a person who does not want to speak about the subject or to hurt you with his point of view about this topic. His words will say that he agrees with you although he thought the opposite. This contradiction will cause the same movements and gestures of self-massages.

Now, you will observe a series of pictures including various postures, movements and gestures of self-massages to have a global view of the lies behaviors.

Before looking at the pictures, we will speak about the inches and the hands in the pockets.

If the hands in the pockets is an ordinary position, it is meaningful about your interlocutor state of mind about the subject you ask about.

When someone hands are fully in the pockets this shows that the person is not very at ease with the situation. He could have a small rotation of his body as if he does not want to face the awkward situation. In your interlocutor head, his limbic brain tries to protect itself from the situation.

The hands in the pockets with the arisen inches, is often the sign of a self confident and determined person. For example a trustful person, who says the truth, will not try to flee the situation, or to hide, he will face the situation.

The third way it is to put only the inches in the pockets. This position of the hands like for the hands, which are completely in the pockets, betrays an embarrassment. He wants to give the impression of being relaxed but the situation makes him uncomfortable.

He may be relaxed but after the embarrassing question you asked him, you could observe this gesture, added to the body rotation to avoid confrontation.

As we speak about movements, when someone lies he will keep in the background (the prey) and will have a manner of moving which will go in the same direction. He will have slow and small movements. Conversely, someone who says the truth will look at you right in your eyes and accompanies his words by dynamic gestures, which will give weight to his arguments.

A liar will have an evasive glance; he will not look at you directly in the eyes. In this book, we will practice to take liar place. Do you look at your interlocutor in his eyes when you lie (I think that you already did it)? It is difficult, especially when it is about a delicate situation.

Even if you are able to do it one second, you will avert your glance, in your head, you say yourselves, "I will not look him in his eyes so that he should not discover the truth". In fact, everyone detects intuitively when you lie to him, not because he is able to read in your eyes but precisely because you avert them. maybe he shames to lie to you!

Let us return a small second to the full movements that a person carries out to give weight to his arguments. Conversely, someone who is out of tune with he says, will have discrete and tiny movements.

Observe the following picture:

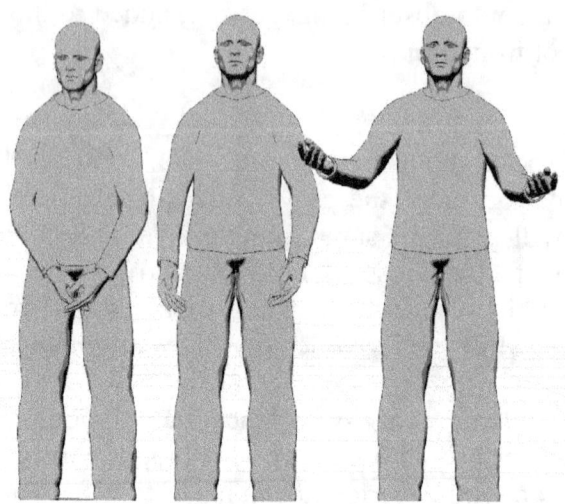

The first person has a closed position, to protect himself with his arms by his sides and his hands joined. That expresses a kind of ill-being.

Then, you can observe two different openings, the first one is from someone who lies and who wants to give the impression to argue by making small movements with his hands, but his elbows remain stuck as if he was afraid to reveal the truth if he will open out them (I must say, to reveal the lie). It is often to see this kind of behavior in broadcasts.

On the set, A guest seated on a chair, which does not believe at all in what he says (or lies to say more simply what he think) he forces himself to do little arms movements with his statement. He does that to simulate to give weight to his arguments in order to be convincing, but his gestures will be small, slow and unobtrusive.

Often, you will observe that his hands move and his arms stay fixed.

Have you ever seen someone impassioned by his subject who

speaks as much as he moves his hands and his arms? This person probably says the truth because he puts all his heart into what he says and wants to argue strongly with full and dynamic movements like the third person on the picture.

Imagine you to ask a direct question to your interlocutor in which you accuse him wrongly to be a liar, do you think that he will huddle down or try to hide or avert his glance?

And you, if you are accused wrongly how will you react? Will you fix your interlocutor or will you support all your words by gestures or will you give up before the truth springs?

Which is the gesture of protection that we all know and that you often apply to protect you without learned it? No need to describe it, it is when we cross our arms. During talks between friends or colleagues, you ask or another person asks an indiscreet question, do you never realize that suddenly you cross your arms?

You watch two people in the train, they talk about this and that and suddenly one of them crosses quickly his arms. You can easily deduce that he is now in an uncomfortable situation.

We can compare this gesture to a need of comfort, but when we lie, we manage to stand aloof from our interlocutor. If you start your conversation by "I would like to speak about this subject" and your interlocutor suddenly crosses his arms and says:"ok no problem, I am at ease with this subject" at this moment, you can expect that the words he will says will be out of tune with his thoughts.

Here on the following photo a traditional position which consists, for the liar, in protecting himself from the attacks:

Crossed hands as we can see on the picture, shows a certain unrest considering a given situation. The professional players of poker try, when they notice their adversaries to adopt this gesture, to see with which pressure their fingers are tight in order to determine the level of stress and thus the extend of the bluff which they are creating.

However, the following picture indicates the opposite. The hands are joined but the fingers are not crossed, they form a kind of arrow upwards. A self-confident person has an upright posture, unlike someone who is not at ease and tries to hide himself.

This position of the fingers joined and pointing to the top can be associated with the concept to have an upright posture or to move upwards.

Therefore, attention this picture represents a person who faith in what she says.
Now, the last picture shows the concept of protection that someone who lies will adopt.

It represents a sort of shield between her and her interlocutor and thinks that she is protected and he cannot see that she lies.

This posture as all the others will of course be preceded by a limbic reaction, most of the time they will be following with an evasive glance, particularly when it is lies' turn to speak".

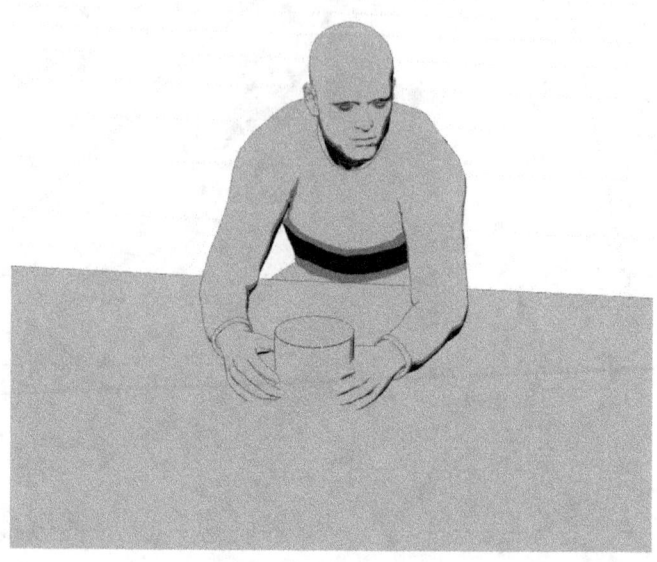

On this last image, the person takes whatever came to hand to interpose it between her and you like a shield. We can observe this protective behaviour during a job interview.

According the pictures, you grasp the notion of "space occupation" or "how to take a prominent position during a discussion". We will study the case of someone who "is questioned" and must answer questions, what's more, he has not dinner by candlelight.

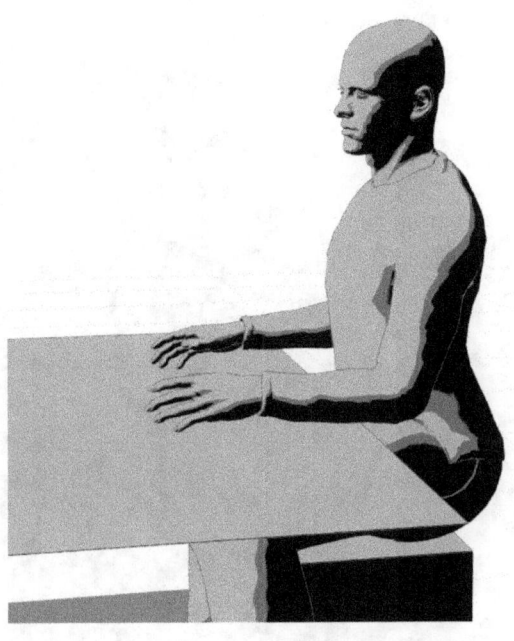

This image represents the "normal" position of a sited person who is at ease. His arms are put on the table, in opened position, not cross and do not touch them.

If you ask a question that surprises him and makes him start a limbic reaction, which shows that this question implies him, then it will occur certainly a space movement backwards.

On the following picture, this person will hide, move away, and protect herself from this threat, with the gestures of which we spoke before (gestures of protections).

If he is in no way to blame he will remain relaxed, he will argue his words by full gestures to give more weight to them, to occupy more space.

During a poker party, someone who occupies space at the poker table is a trustful person, who has a good hand and does not need to hide a bluff.

Here is an example of space occupation.

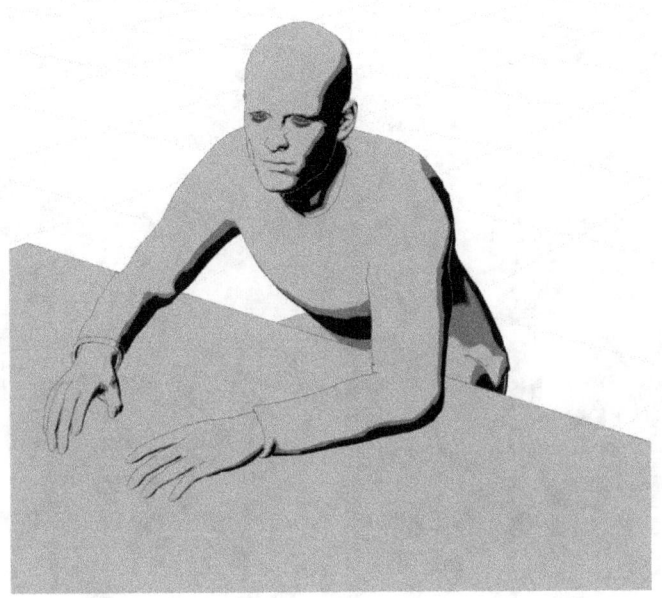

As I introduced it in this chapter, a common movement of protection is to turn your body to the threat. For example when you play football, (I am sure you usually made it) you attack your opponent in a profile and not a full frontal way!

Even if you are sitting or standing, the position is the same. Often, unconscious hope to escape is linked with this movement.

Here is an example :

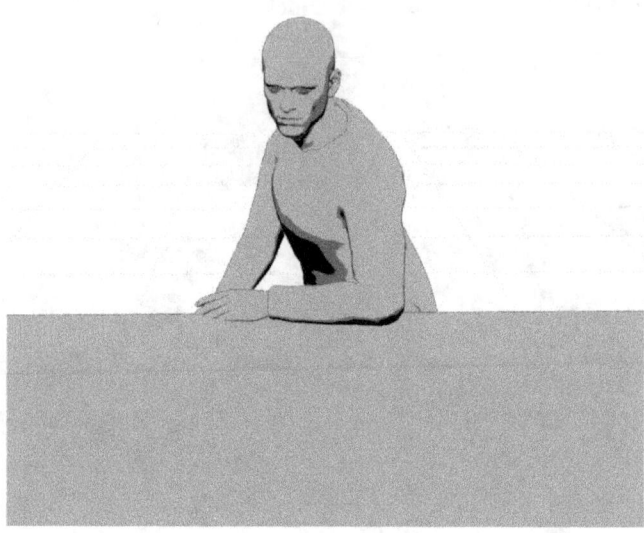

Now that we broached the concepts of space and protection, we will speak about these famous self-massages that I touch on at the beginning of this chapter.

Here are some pictures that refer to the self-massages. I am sure that you already made some of them without realizing.

You certainly observed several times, the classic movement,
which consists in massing the nape of the neck. Let us continue…

Another classic gesture is to massage our ear lobe, I am sure you already noticed it.

Then….

This gesture "two in one" represents two things, on the one hand a massage of the brow and on the other hand, the fact of hiding the glance, as not to be affected by what occurs.

We can think that a person in this position is thinking but in fact, he rather tries to hide something.

Other gesture that you already made is to scrape your nose, or rather to massage it. You often observed it among your interlocutors.

Let's observe the following picture:

The position of the thinker… well, maybe he massages his chin! I often observed this position in poker or chess game. That can be a technique to dissimulate a part of our face in order to be discrete, over and above the fact that he can stabilize his head if he is too much stressed. If in spite of that you note a self-massage behind this position, something occurred to him.

The fact of hiding the mouth with the hand, or to put one or two fingers to our mouth, can be also interpreted as a will to dissimulate information, or to keep silent.

In the newspaper or on Internet it is very easy to find photographs of people making these gestures…

Here is another example that you have already pointed out:

The massage of the chin, the fist is closed but the inch under the chin takes part in this massage.

Your interlocutor position can be compared to someone thinking, but it is not the case especially if you observe a massage made with the fingers or the inch under the chin.

In the last picture….

There is a very common movement of self-massage, maybe you have never paid attention to it, there is about a more or less wide massage of your forearm with your inch. We can add that this position is close to the cross arms one, as to hinder to keep his distance.

To conclude this chapter, the main points to remember are:

1 - The different limbic reactions and the space movements associated

2 - The self-massages

3 - And the fact that it's not really necessary for you to rush at your interlocutor if you detect a lie but rather you must pay attention to that at the precise moment when his gestures joined his words, his thoughts were not in line with his behavior and words.

Now you will be able to note the incredible number of self-massages gestures among your interlocutors and the people you will meet. To do that you do not need to memorize thousand techniques.

You will observe woman who play with their necklace or locket straight after an embarrassing question; you will observe among man who loosen their ties or pull down their tee-shirt collar as to slacken a tended situation. Nevertheless, the main part of the self-massages is on the body as you have just seen it throughout this chapter.

Let us approach now a different and subtle register in…

Chapter 5

LIES, LOGIC AND COMMON SENSE

Do you think that it is possible to detect lies without using the techniques that we saw in the preceding chapters? Is it possible to detect them, only by listening to the words that leave the mouth of somebody?

Yes indeed! It is precisely the topic that we are going to speak in this chapter, is based mainly on the answers of your interlocutors.

In fact, it is about logic and common sense in the way of creating answers although the origin of these answers is from an obvious psychological mechanism.

You can used these techniques alone, but they constitute an additional arsenal to rank carefully in your lie detector toolbox. Therefore, if you want to be more effective you can combine them with the "limbic" techniques, of which we spoke in the preceding chapters.

However, those techniques can help you to detect lies in different situations as when you have phone conversation and cannot see your interlocutor for example. I really say to help you; to give you some clues about the real the intentions of your interlocutor.

Last point, these techniques are not at all difficult, they are easy to memorize and locate in the discussions, but to understand them still more deeply, you must try throughout this chapter to
put yourselves to the lies' shoes. What would you do if you were the liar?

Are you ready? Then let us come straight to the point.

The art of sidestepping.

Someone who is surprised by an awkward question and intend to lie will be under pressure and the most natural thing that he will try to do, is to elude from it, to move away. The first technique used by the liar will be to fight shy of subject!

There are more or less subtle ways to change subject and maybe you will meet people who excel at this practice. There are different practises;

- The direct manner, your interlocutor will simply change subject when you ask him the fateful question.

- The opportunist manner is when an external event, having no connection with your discussion, emerges at this specific time as the phone ringing, something occurring in the street or anything that allows your interlocutor to change subject.

- The subtle manner is to take one element of your question in order to change or to divert the conversation onto this element. Let us take an example, you lent money to your friend and without being abrupt you ask him "on the way back from my mother home, I remembered that you owed me money so could you tell me when you think pay me back? ».

One of the possible answer is: "well, I will give you soon news about it, I have to check two or three tricks, well, what about your mother, how is she? " etc etc….or "guess what I met on the road a few moments ago, I saw this..., so I did that, and I felt that..." etc etc…

Another indirect way to proceed is to use an element belonging to your life by someone who knows you very well. If we take the last example, the answer could be "by the way, do you have news about the exam you took last week? Do you pass it? ".

Well, I think that you understood the principle; the changing of subject is the principal technique used by liars to get round an embarrassing question.

Ok, suppose you are a liar, you made a stupid thing, and the person concerned with your silly thing comes to asks you an embarrassing question. Just after your limbic reaction you will be in a continuous state of stress" and your unique goal now will be to eliminate this stress and to leave this situation. What are you going to do? You will arrange things so that to change subject.

In the chapter "tactics and strategies" we will see how to effectively trap someone who changes subject. It does not matter whether he does it directly or subtly as long as you notice that he has change the subject.

Variable-geometry answers

The differences in the types of answers that your interlocutors can give you could be important. It depends on if they tell you lies or the truth. I also call that the answers with various levels of depths, if you analyze them, they will give you a precise idea about the reality of the facts presented.

For that, let's take an example of the real life.

Your spouse call you on the phone right before leaving her job to tell you that she go to a party with her friends and she will be back in the night. Once returned, you ask her if she had a pleasant evening.

She answers: "oh, yes, good".

You will note that this answer misses details, all the more so if you surprised her by asking the question at a moment she didn't expect it. You already hear it said that liars give little details about their stories. It is true, and it is important to understand why.

Nevertheless, let me broach an important point, when you hear someone giving to you answers you must take his behaviour account.

Or, to be more precise, how she is used to answer and how she answers you right now. For example, usually she spends thirty minutes to tell about her evening and now she answers you only by "Oh it was pleasant".

Then, why someone who lies does not go into details? Put yourselves in her shoes, you return the evening from the party and your spouse asks you "how was your evening?" You answer simply "Oh it was well", she does not insist. On the other hand, the following day during the breakfast she starts the conversation "Well, tell me about your last evening…"

You are surprised; do you think you can create a whole story in no time at all? Definitely not.
I do not think it is possible, and what immediately will cross your mind?

Something like "Oh it was very nice", it is easy, fast to output and no need to use your brain.
If it is the truth, do not worry, it will be easy for you to tell her what you did last evening because you lived it. The secret of this technique is in the fact that it is very difficult to invent immediately a whole story, and what is more coherent and the following answers of level two typify it.

Let us return to our story when your spouse answered you, as it is not enough for you, you require more details. Here is a probable answer: "It was very pleasant, we went to a bar to have a drink and after went to the restaurant for a dinner. It was very pleasant".

Even if this story has more details, it is not sufficient. It is easy to invent and prepare in advance this kind of answer.

Indeed, from the liar point of view, it is easy to remember and there is less chance to make a mistake or to be incoherent. Thus, in this present case, we should suggest the possibility that this answer is not the reflection of the truth.

Let's analyze this type of answer: "oh, it was very pleasant, we went to have a drink then we went to the restaurant, so-and-so were present and we laughed all the evening". What do you think about it? According to you, is it the truth or a lie?

Yet, this answer has more details than the two preceding ones. Let me tell you that the liars always create stories with positive events. Things are running smoothly in their stories, there are practically never negative things.

Why? Because it is easier to say positive thing than negative one, "It was pleasant, they were sympathetic, things are running smoothly" than "oh it was deadly dull, it went off badly». Do not forget that you lie and if you answer negative things, your interlocutor will ask you more questions to gain a deeper understanding of what happened. Therefore, as many answers were invented, do you think that the liars want to get caught out by his spouse? In addition, if you mix positive and negative points you strongly increase the chances to make a mistake or to contradict yourself.

Therefore, what do you think about this answer? Is it a lie or the truth? There is every chance that it is an invented reply; an answer memorized in the case you should ask her more questions. If you have doubts, ask other questions and analyze the answers again. Are they of the same build?

First and foremost, take the fourth level of answer into account. Imagine the following answer: "Ah it was very pleasant, we went to have a drink, and then we went to the restaurant.
So-and-so was there, his wife too; she was delighted to see me again after all these years. She said to me that she was happy to have changed job and she felt better now".

Would be you able to invent a similar history without making mistake and without worried stiff to contradict yourself or after several days, she asks again to repeat it?

What is the difference between this answer and the three previous ones? The details, of course but there are other things. Did you notice that he spoke about thoughts, mood or feelings belonging to the other?

For a person who lies, it is very difficult to invent feelings of other interlocutors in a story made up from beginning to end. Try to create one and see how it is difficult not to mention
to be with someone who can detect the lies, in this case she would certainly attacked all your story's sides, which forced to invent more and more answers. Inevitably, you would make mistake or contradict yourself even if you learned the answers by heart and you switch from a very detailed answers to something like "oh it was well". In addition, you will be glad of a chance to change the subject, will not you.

It is one of the reasons because the liars never go into details when they lie. They do not be aware of that but it is a very difficult mental exercise.

Then you will conclude that this fourth answer is certainly the truth.

Here are additional elements will enable you to analyze the depth of an answer from your interlocutor and put forward serious doubts about the veracity of his answers.

Robotization.

Robotization, is a type of answer given by the liar, you certainly heard during your discussions. It is when a liar takes your own words used in your question and he builds his answer with them.

Here is an example: "did you do that?" you could have this kind of answer "No, I didn't do that". Another question: "have you ever thought to be unfaithful to me?" he can answer: "no, I have never thought to be unfaithful to you".

Do you understand the principle? However, this "robotization" is not the ultimate technique of detection; you can add it to the other tools you already collected.

This type of oral answer works better if you surprise your interlocutor, because for him the urgency becomes to find quickly an answer. What is the fastest way to find an answer? It is to take again the words used in the question. If we can read in his thoughts, we will see something like "dammit! Why does she ask me this question now? I must find something to answer immediately! I found, I just have to take the words of her question they will give more weight to my answer! ».

They are very useful these actions in slow motion, are not they?

May I help you?

If you blame someone wrongly, what do you think he will do? Do you think he will get hide or to stay silent? Certainly not, rather the reverse, this person will do everything to convince you that he is not or did not do what you said. He will look you straight in the eye, asking you with firm voice and full and dynamic gestures until you will understand that he is innocent.

This behaviour is the opposite of the point number one that we spoke about at the beginning of this chapter, which is about change of subject. An innocent person will not change subject, on the contrary, he will hang on to it.

Let us take another example. You work in a company and every day you park your car on the places reserved. When you back home, you realize with horror that you have a dent on your back door! This can be arrived today or yesterday. The following day you decide to investigate to your colleagues.

To be simple, let us imagine that you have only two colleagues. You question the first by using the allusion technique (we will speak about it in the next chapter). "I think there is someone here who parks his car like a savage who has no regard for other people's property and hammers at the door; do you know how we could settle this problem? ».

According to the fact that you speak to the guilty or not you will see different behaviours, the attitude of one or the other will be singularly different. If you ask the guilty, you will be able to see all the signals that he will produce. On the other hand, if you ask an innocent person, what do you think he is going to do? And you, what would you do?

It is all the opposite of the person who will do everything to change subject, you will sympathize for the victim, you will easily discuss about this subject, you even propose your assistance. Now, put yourself in guilty place imagine that you really did that. How will you react? Do you discuss quietly about the subject? It is too risked and you could betray yourself.

To conclude this point, now you know that someone who lies will not linger on a subject unlike the innocent person who will not hesitate to approach and offer you some help. To analyze this behaviour it is an important clue in the detection of the lies.

Art to play for time.

Why do we play for time? To think of the lies which the liar will give you?

"Why do you tell me that?", "I am sorry but I don't understand your question", "Excuse me, could you repeat your question?" Can you be more precise? ", "I think that we know both the answer", "do you ask me about this? " What? ", "excuses me, but I was concentrated on what I did".

Have you never heard this kind of answers?

When you question someone, sorry, when you ask your interlocutor a question, which surprised him, one of the techniques used by the liars, is to try to gain time. This time helps him to create lie. Psychologically speaking, it is a way to stomach the surprise, surprise means emotion, which caused a limbic reaction, with different gestures, movements, glance, self-massage, etc … you know the continuation.

You have just to observe, take notes and wait quietly the oral answer. Now you have a good clue, which is playing for time.

Generalization.

Generalization is a way for the liar, to change the subject in order to find a loophole.

For example, to the question: "have you ever thought to be unfaithful to me?" what do you think about this answer: "well you know, it is not in my practices to do that, I have a moral conscience". Or, this other answer: "people who do that are totally amoral. I do not understand how they can do it".

This type of answer has three effects,

1 – To give the impression that he (the liar) is a moral person and he does not usually do that.

2 – To parade his morality can also make you feel guilty, indeed, how could you challenge your spouse integrity?
3 – To throw a tantrum when you ask her the question is also a way to change the subject and try to frighten you so you will never ask her an embarrassing question.
It is the third limbic reaction, aggressiveness contrary to the fact of freezing or avoiding.

The third effect helps to change discreetly the subject and the fact of speaking about general information creates a diversion and then sidesteps the question.

The combination of these three effects (change of the subject, to make someone guilty and morality parade) sow doubts in your mind and convinces you that all would be well. We saw that the change of subject was the principal action of a liar to escape the pressure, which hangs over his head.

You will note the number of people who sidestep the question to answer the questions. It is simply amazing. Television is swarming with some people who during interviews use it because they do not want to recognize that they are wrong, or lie purely and simply.

Let us take a fact, which occurred during the interview of a personality. An international business was not resolved because France did not have relations with the country in question.
The journalist asks him "why couldn't you solve this problem? If I understood France has no co-operation with this country?"

What do you think he answered? Did he answer yes or not? Did he recognize this weakness?
No, he answered, "France is connected with more than 80 countries and our government attaches a great importance to these relations which make possible to solve this kind of problems". He managed to wriggle out of the situation. Nevertheless, if we analyze his response, we can pick out the 3 points:

1- Morality, France is in relation to….great importance…

2- Culpability, maybe I am wrong to criticize my country,

3- Here we are witness to someone who sidesteps the question, a way to change the subject.

I let you try…

The pursuit of approval

Your interlocutor could try to found approval; he will check if you swallowed hook, line and sinker.

Maybe you have already heard someone who after told you his story wanted to know if you believed him (with a question like: »you believe me, don't you? »). Sometimes a liar who needs your approval looks you straight in the eye to see if you believed him.

Whereas during a good part of the lie he spoke with downcast, do not make a mistake about the fact she looks you straight in the eye, it is just to see if you believe her lie and not because she said the truth. Here just asked a question and she did not need to lie.

We will see advanced techniques of lies in the following chapters in keeping the eyes, as well as techniques of counter-attacks, as for example to answer her "yes, I believe you" to manage to slip her.

If someone tells you, "do you believe me?" you probably ask a liar who needs to ascertain that you believe his lie. Or misses self-confidence, therefore, keep this clue aside and made
the link with those you already collected.

To be honest with you.

If you meet someone who begins his sentences with «to be honest with you", or: "to tell you the truth", or: "to be frank… " you must pay attention to what he says because whether he lied or he going to lie.

To be on the defensive

A liar can be on the defensive and his answers lack details, which could sow doubts in your mind. Here are some "weapons" to add to your arsenal.

Let's play a little game in three examples.

According to you, who is the liar?

A man goes to a store after-sales service, the computer he just bought does not work, so he wants his money back. The salesman, takes the computer, plugs in it but nothing, the computer doesn't start. He opens the computer and discovers that a component misses: "But, the hard disk misses! ».

Two cases could be evoked, first case, he is innocent, second case he stole the hard disk.

Here is his answer: "Ah, it is not me, it was like this when I bought the machine! ».

Then? innocent or guilty?

Here is another answer of the man: "What! I spent all my time to wonder why it doesn't work to be this is the cause of the problem? What a waste of time! "

Do you find out who stole the hard disk?

Second example.

Three technicians work in a company to service a machine, they use the car of the company they park it just beside the boss car. However, one day the boss notices a large impact on his right door, the side of the employees' car. Furious, the following day he calls the three employees.

The boss asks, "yesterday someone dented my door car and it is your side door, do you know what occurred? ».

Answer 1: I am sorry, but if I did that, I would immediately come to inform you.

Answer 2: don't ask me about that because I always pay attention to this kind of things.

Answer 3: I am upset, could you tell me if the impact is important? That already happened to me too and it is not pleasant.

According to you, who put a blow of door in the boss car?

Third example:

You have two children, the weather is hot, you went away to do the shopping and one of your children ate the last ice cream that you reserved for you! You ask your children for a meeting in the living room!

Your question: "Who ate the last ice-cream?"

The answers could be:

1- What? Does remain no more ice cream in the freeze? I wanted one!"

2- It was not me; this morning I did not go into the kitchen.

According to you, who ate the last ice cream?

It is the typical answers that you can obtain from people who are on the defensive. It is a matter of obvious signals, gestures, glances or anything we have already seen in the other chapters, it just about a defensive answer which helps you to find out who ate the ice cream…

Of course, if you add the limbic reactions, the gestures, the self-massages, the eyes orientation, you can unearth the truth.

With some practices, (still and always) you can in this type of cases to discover instantaneously who did what, who lies or who says the truth. Then, who lied in our example?

In the computer case, the liar is the first man. Sometimes it could be easy to discover the truth and sometimes it could be difficult. Let us dissect the action…

The liar is on the defensive and usually his first words are "it is not me", "don't require me about that", "it was in this state when I found it" etc etc…

The liar always justifies himself, tries to convince you that he says the truth, which allows him to change the subject. Another important point is that liars' answers are dispassionately "impersonal", on the contrary to the answer of the other man (the innocent) who is focused on the time he lost and does not worry to express his feelings and to speak more and more.

Then, who damaged the boss' car?

As you guessed it is the second employee, you can discover it according the elements we have already seen. The liar practices a generalization of the things to create a diversion. Now it will be easy for you to know who will eat the last ice cream. The liar is the second child one.

He was on the defensive, tried to justify himself on the opposite of the first child who was worried about the fact that it did not remain any ice cream (do you noted the emotion).

I am sure that you already answered like this when you made silly things...

Now, you have tools, which will allow you to shine out the truth or to collect lot of clues.
They can be useful to you even when you do not see your interlocutor. However do not conclude too fast; wait until you collect enough clues for the confrontation which will be easier.

Let us stop discussing; now you will enter in the cutthroat world of manipulation, strategy and the tactics to mastering the art of counter-attack, so, you will lead this world!

Welcome in…

Chapter 6

TACTICS, STRATEGIES AND
COUNTER-ATTACK

Suppose that you are in a critical situation and you intend to do battle in order that the truth come out into the open.

OK! I heard you, but before, to take no chances, I'll teach you to become an expert in the art of building psychological traps, so that you should lock your interlocutors in a soft and invisible cage in which they can no longer extricate themselves once they realize it. But stop raving, you could not lock up your interlocutor in a windowless room, tied him up to a chair with a unique blinding lamp pointed to his face and ask him all the questions you want?

Well if this idea might cross your mind, it is not possible!

But psychologically, it is possible to create a similar situation in your interviewer mind, and all without he realizes it!

We will study this, later in this chapter with a concrete example.

That is the challenge of this chapter, to turn you into a skilled person in detecting lies. As you know, the surprise is the most effective way to induce limbic reactions.

Two things emerge from what we just discussed, the first one is to prepare the ground to create a surprise.

The second one, which is not absolutely necessary, is to set an invisible trap to discourage him to lie, so he will have the impression that he felt into this trap and all his attempts to escape will be an evidence of his guilt which will force him to confess to you.

How to prepare the ground ?

You must take no chances to create the most limbic reactions from your partner. The first thing to do, is don't change your habits. If your friend is a little paranoid, he will see the slightest change in your habits. Some people do not see anything that happen around them while others observe everything they will notice any change in your behavior. If you do not usually talk about some subjects and suddenly you start to talk about them, you might arouse suspicions. We will see that latter when we will broach the subject about "attack by allusions".

Do not change anything, do what you usually do, in the same way.

Do not tell your partner before leaving for work: "we need to talk about something" or "tonight we'll have to discuss." You prepare your fight, not his! Put yourself in front of a bull (dressed in red) and gesticulate like a fury so you get the same result …

Time is your best ally, any precipitation could also be interpreted as a change of habit. So, do not try to precipitate things, use an event already plan (like a dinner in a restaurant) and build your trap. A pleasant place, is the best way to win his trust, so you can really surprise him and create the most limbic reactions. You must, therefore, and this will be the second point, create a favourable environment to be quit confident and your friend should feel at ease, be easy in his mind. To establish this, you will need to be yourself in this state of mind. I know that it can be difficult to do that if you plan to speak about a delicate subject but, gestures and postures we will talk about will help you.

Try do not be on the defensive, adopt an open posture (ie the opposite of closed positions that we have already talked about in terms of postures and behaviors).

Do not keep your distance with your arms folded, approach, occupy space geographically. Do not insert any objects between you and him, give him the impression that every thing is all right and that you are happy to be right here with him.

You can mimic the postures of your contact, Have you ever noticed that when you are with someone, you often take the same posture, without realizing it?

You do this is because you feel comfortable with this person, it is called the empathy technique. Well, use this technique to win your partner's trust, take sometimes the same position, the same posture that him. You will transmit him a feeling of well being, he will feel good in your company without realizing it. He must drop his guard, do not forget that it is a strategy of manipulation, not a candlelight dinner!

Let's review the situation, to be efficient in the art of detecting lies, you must surprise your partner and to get this surprise you have to prepare the ground. This will serve you for all the attacks we will discuss later, whether for a simple situation or a difficult situation. Difficult situations may require the use of psychological trap strategy that we talked about (in this chapter) and a good ground preparation is the foundations of a solid construction!

This requires that you do not change your habits, you create a relaxed atmosphere, and don't forget to be relaxed yourself to make him drop his guard. Introducing now a notion, indeed a tool that will be of great use when you launch your attack, because in this chapter, you will not remain passive in the face of any better still you will become an attacker.

This tool is linked to time and it can be described as the art of putting pressure on your interlocutor for a short moment. The name of this tool is: silence!

More than a tool it is a powerful weapon that you will use repeatedly in your discussions with the others. Silence is one of the most powerful words. Indeed, liars have a strong aversion to silence. It produces a feeling of unease, a feeling of suffocation that can provoke new reactions.

We will not go deeper into the advantage because we will use it in the first attack of this chapter:

The direct attack.
As you can imagine it, the technique of direct attack is to talk directly about the problem. This technique has its advantages, but also has significant drawbacks. In fact, two cases arise immediately under a direct attack. First case, your interlocutor is innocent and you accused him wrongly.

Everything depends on the relation you have with this person, but this attack could cast a chill over your relation, then it is better for you to have strong suspicions before using a direct attack.

Second case, the person is guilty. The advantage of this direct technique is that if you have prepared the ground you can see many limbic and behavioral reactions, gestures, words and post-limbic reactions.

Well done, however the disadvantage is that he could become aggressive. Therefore, you saw in the previous chapter the techniques which will help you to draw the good conclusions (the different types of responses, the change of subject etc. etc. ...).

To be on the defensive or to be aggressive show that your interlocutor is involved in the topic you speak with him and even feel threatened. Don't forget that the disadvantage of this attack is that the person will become defensive, and not only now but all the time and the next time you will ask him another question he may prepare in advance his answers. But don't worry we'll soon see how to dissect these answers.

Let's take an actual instance, you expect the return of your daughter at home, and you suspect her to smoke.

Ground preparation:

Don't change your habits, wait until she comes back from school, welcome her ,as you usually do and take a relaxed attitude. If you used to welcoming her on the doorstep, clasping her in your arms and telling her "how was your day?", You can instead say her quietly in the ear: "so you smoke now ?" and calmly look her straight in the eye in a great and long silence.

Of course, it is when you ask your question that you have put into practice all the detection techniques that you learned in previous chapters. In this example we more focus on the attack itself, but we must not forget the detection! This technique will work very well the first time, but your daughter will now distrust you and then, will wondering when you will set a trap for her.

This can have two effects, either to persuade her not to lie or, she will try to better cover up her future lies. You can adapt this technique without any problems to all scenarios, but don't forget the drawbacks.

If your friend has already prepared his answers or if he has a suspicion about your intentions, or knows that you doubt him, particularly since he regularly went out in the the evening with his "friends" whereas before he did not ? He think that it has necessarily aroused your suspicion and now, he expect your question. Well, you'll learn how to dissect learned answer much more quickly than the customs officer disassembling a car for drugs.

You can even use them against your interlocutor.

It is a very funny game (depending on the situation of course) which can be practiced sitting quietly in your chair. The first point to consider is the eyes direction. Because the liar has memorized his answer, there's a good chance that his eyes direction will be false. So please note it but does not consider it as the truth. Second step is the ground, now you know the tactics, if his favorite position is to be seated comfortably (as the example above) in his armchair, so, wait for the moment when he is the more relaxed, maybe when he will sip his favorite drink, or he will lunch. Then ask him the same question like last time.

If you have already prepared the ground you will detect the signs, because you'll surprise him and there will the reactions. Even if he had prepared his response.

This time you daughter will reply: "What? What are you talking about, I do not smoke, you can ask my friends, then anyway, it is bad for health ". You can detect in her answer an attempt to save time ("what?") to put up with the surprise and perhaps to remember the invented answer. Do you notice the generalization ("it is bad for your health")? Now you have a beautiful sentence, as beautiful as a pizza from the oven. You just have to play.

To begin let's her finish her sentence, don't say anything, for a while don't breathe a word so observe new reactions.

Then tell her: "Really?".

Be in wait for new reactions and keep silent for a moment. I think you will detect a lot of signs of lie just by uttering a single word!

But it's not over, now it will become more fun. Indeed! The more the liar will prepare his answers the more you will find elements to reverse the situation. You have just to take each element of the response and to use them against her.

In this example you can say " so, you do not smoke ?" Followed by a brief silence, then: "So, I can go see your friends and ask them?".

Go on saying, "do you really think it's unhealthy to smoke?". If she does not smoke she gladly continue the conversation conversely if she is under pressure, because you're about to discover the truth, she will try to change the subject. While it is easy to invent a sentence and memorize it, it will become impossible to predict the path that will take the conversation and to invent all the answers.

Reverse the situation and imagine yourself being questioned in the same way, with times of heavy silences and all the questions including the elements of your lie! put yourself one second in her shoes? Your mother asks you this question: "But the other day when I put your clothes in the machine there was a smell of cigarettes, what do you think about that?". Can you really invent a detailed response right now?

Attention, I still remember that the goal is for each question you ask, to detect signs of lying, and not to force your daughter to orally admit her lies, do not forget it. The psychological pressure is a little later in this chapter …

Your daughter will do everything to try to change the subject, then let's study the technique that will enable you to effectively counter attack this attempt.

There are two ways to counter a change of subject, a radical, and an underhand one. Well that's all I have in stock ... The radical way is: when your interlocutor changes the subject, stop him immediately. You can tell him: "Do not change the subject and answer to my question".

This has the effect of adding an extra pressure, because the change of subject is really the solution that the liar will absolutely look for to disentangle him from this situation. And as long as he can not escape, the pressure will increase and if there is pressure there is emotion (stress), then the limbic brain will react, then ... you know the rest.

The sneaky way to proceed is to let your partner change the subject. Let him talk about the new discussion topic for a while, but, focus on his behavior. Since he changed the subject is he more relaxed? can you see a change in his posture or his position, was he collapsed on the sofa as if he feels comfortable?

Were his arms crossed before he change the subject?

In fact any posture which switches from closed to open. If he is relaxed, (and he probably is) is because the pressure has disappeared. And if the pressure is gone, you can deduce that before there was far more pressure, so a state of stress, and therefore a lie or an attempt to hide something.

But that's not the funniest of the sneaky technique because now that your interlocutor is relaxed, you can start talking again about this sensitive subject, when you do that you create a double pressure. First, you will surprise him again, and second, he would not appreciate having to deal again with this subject. There will be new limbic reactions, believe me!

This type of emotional changing, moving from a state of stress to relax and a few time later moving from relax to a state of stress can be difficult to manage and even your interlocutor will own up to lying. Must I remind you that it was not the purpose of this technique.

As we are in the "pressurized" phase, let's studies the following technique which will allow you to increase this pressure.

To succeed with this technique you must practice to detect lies. Some techniques must become conditioned reflexes because the aim of these techniques is to put continuous pressure on your interlocutor. We must destabilize him, not giving him time to react, drive him to make most errors to reveal most lies signals. You'll make him realized that you are able to detect lies and so add pressure. Let's see an example to understand all the key points. Do not forget the ground preparation of course.

Consider again the case of your daughter who started to smoke. You have prepared the ground, she is drinking his favorite soda in the sofa while watching television.

This is an example but you can adapt it to your personal situation. You enter the lounge with a chair in your hand. You put the chair in front of your daughter and you sit. You're very close to your daughter, now she can not see the TV, only you!

Here is a trick, when you sit straddle your chair and put your arms on the chair back. This position has a deterrent effect on your interlocutor who has the feeling that you're protected by a shield and that you can not be touched.

So, tell her::
YOU: "so you started to smoke?"
Your daughter: "What? What are you talking about? "
YOU: "Do not tell me what! you have understood, do not play for time to think about the lie that you will get out!"
Your daughter: "But no! I do not smoke! " she said as she is massaging her ear lobe.
YOU: "Oh! There, you've just massaged your ear lobe, people who lie mass their ear. You can point the finger at her lobe to add more pressure.
Your daughter: "But I told you that I do not smoke!" She said this time looking at you in profile with her arms folded.
You: "But your body and your face are telling me the opposite now, you don't dare to look me straight in the eye, you are massaging your arm, these are signs of lies. And you know what, I am not telling you everything".
You: "Well I know enough stuff, I thought as much!, I'll think about your punishment."
Then you exit the room. If your daughter does not say a word when you leave the room you have the final confirmation that she probably smokes, otherwise she would follow you and do her utmost to convince you that she is innocent.

The main objective of this technique is to provoke the show of lies signals, because of this constant pressure, but it can also make her to confess the truth.
But there again, good ground preparation is like to build a solid foundation to a building. It is the best way to urge someone to have the most reactions.

We will now enter the exciting world of the furtive attacks, or the art of detecting lies without arousing suspicion.
To do this we will use an attack called the allusion. There are several ways to make allusions and that is precisely what we are going to talk.

The general allusion.

Lets take the following scenario: You suspect your spouse having an affair. Like for the other points we have already discussed, let me remind you that a good ground preparation is the key to success. The allusion is a kind of test, you will set a trap to see if your interlocutor will rise to the bait. This is the most discreet technique to gather information. For example, during a dinner you could talk your boyfriend about something you saw on television.

YOU: "I saw a very interesting television programme about couple relationships, there was opinion poll to know if they had people who they have already deceived their spouses. And you know what? 50% of them have already done it! Do you realize that? ".

You understand that during your speech you are in an observation process, you are looking for reactions, especially when you tell him the results! You can increase the pressure by remaining silent for a moment, then ask him: "What do you think about this?".

If your spouse has an affair, the more you'll be long on the subject the more you put pressure on him, and better, ask him about his opinion on this subject he surely prefer to avoid. Because even if you do not give him the impression to have suspicions, he will inevitably take it personally. Adapt this allusion to your situation, especially in ground preparation. If your spouse knows that you often watch TV, or read newspaper or spend time on Internet to stay informed, then he will not see many coincidences between what he wants to keep secret and the subject that you bring to the table.

In this scenario, you could add more pressure starting with a sentence like this: "the other night when you came home late ... I read an article on the Internet .....". In this case it is a double allusion, especially if you think that he was with someone else this specific night.

let's use this scenario, but with a different type of allusion. This is the same process but now you will create an identification of your spouse with a close relation. An example will clarify things:

YOU: " I learned an awful thing this morning I received a call from Ms X and she told me she had discovered that her boyfriend

was unfaithful! Do you realize it ? ".
As in the previous case you're already in "observation" mode from the beginning.

Then, keep silent for a moment (which is a great moment of loneliness for your spouse). Then tell him: "what do you think about that?". You can even add: "It's really disgusting! If I were her I would have kick my boyfriend to the exit direction .... ".

Do you understand the idea of the allusion technique ?

But before moving on to another attack and then move to the ultimate attack that will end this chapter, let's considering the third allusion that I call: the heart attack because it will put a so strong pressure (and so suddenly) that you can not miss the limbic reactions that will follow. And this with just an allusion.
For this technique you have to make a little effort. Imagine that, you have an affair with another woman (or another man), you are unfaithful. Taking the place of the liar is important to understand and feel the effects... Feel free to change the scenario if this one bothers you.

Let's go.
You come home late at night, nothing to report. The next day you come back late at night, then nothing, no suspicion, no questions. Then the next morning at breakfast, still nothing to report. Then comes the moment you eat your sandwich and there still nothing to report. At the last sip of your delicious coffee you enjoy, just as the last drop gently glides along your palate, your wife (the real) tells you: "Oh, tonight I have a nightmare I dreamed that you had slept with another woman.... ". It is a rather direct allusion but this is still an allusion since you're supposed to had a nightmare. However, you will see a festival of limbic reactions and perhaps even see drops of sweat beading on his forehead!

Even more, if you leave a great silence, then a second sentence like this one: "It was so real, this is the first time I have a dream like that".

The technique of allusion is a good way to get information discreetly and has more advantages than the direct attack that we saw previously. It is possible to add it a nuance that you can use in conjunction with it which is the fact to relocate the source of information and to transpose it to another person.

The person you attack directly will think that this is not your fault and that the source of this questioning is elsewhere.

Let's take again the scenario of the cigarette, you could tell your daughter: "I just heard some news that I do not like!" and stay silent a moment, wait until your daughter looks you straight in the eye again, then tell her: "You know, Mrs. X, our upstairs neighbour, she said she saw you smoking yesterday!".

As you can understand, by doing that you put the source on someone else and you lighten your involvement in this accusation. It is a variant, but it can give her a feeling of helplessness. Indeed, as you implicate someone who is external to your family it will be difficult to know if what you say is true, this could have a deterrent effect on her so in this case she could think that she doesn't need to lie to you?

You're not the person who caught her red-handed. To conclude this chapter, we will discuss about a method, more than a technique, which will not be suitable for everyone because it is very offensive. Some of you will find the appropriate method to resolve a difficult situation while others would prefer to attack by allusions like we mentioned before.

It depends on your personality and how you handle things in general. Depending on the situation and its emotional weight, it could be not so obvious. Previously we spoke about the case of the person that you want locked in a dark room, tied to a chair and with a powerful spot light pointed at his face.

Of course you can't do it! But, you can create in the mind of your partner the very unpleasant sensation of being trapped in an interrogation, as if he was tied to a chair, enabled to escape and the only way out could be to confess the truth .

It will be too late for him when he will realize that he really fell into the trap (in fact he will not realise that he is in a trap). We will again take the scenario of the unfaithful spouse, you can of course adapt this technique to your situation.

How psychologically reproduce the room where he will be locked up?

How to reproduce the fact to be tied to a chair?

And what about the lamp?

Must I have one in my pocket? (Here I am teasing you).

First phase, ground preparation, the scene will be a small restaurant, why small?

To unconsciously create an immediate feeling of "compression" to your interlocutor. Try to plan your lunch hour when there are the most people.

For three reasons : the first one is to add pressure (still unconscious) because anyone feels suffocated in a tiny restaurant which is full of people.

The second reason, when you feel more or less be held up by the crowd of clients and in this way it will become impossible to leave the table.

The third one, the fact that the restaurant is crammed full may discourage your partner to make a public scandal to try to escape that pressure.

When he will sit in this restaurant he will be in the position of being tied to a chair in a room where it will be difficult to escape. Except that he will not be conscious of it…

Today is the D day, you're in the restaurant, as expected in the first phase, you booked in advance (It is better to be in the driving seat) and took care he sits down at a place from which it is difficult to escape.

You have just to finish the ground preparation as we have already seen in the other points. Keep yourself, proceed as you used to do in a restaurant, then add the chameleon techniques to win your interlocutor trust.

Don't forget the opening techniques. Take your time before to launch an offensive against him. Ideally, he went to the toilet once just to foresee how it is difficult to extricate himself from the table.

I assure you that it will increase the psychological pressure at the right time.

Now It is time to attack ?

To have a more psychological impact, consider the example of the nightmare allusion announced in the previous example exactly when he drinks his coffee, here you can wait the moment where he put his food in his mouth. It is not required to do that, but there is a precise timing to do more damage. We must wait when someone is engaged in a process, even as automatic as that of chewing food.

When you launch the attack, your interlocutor will be really surprised and stressed, as he is about to swallow his food will have a better effect (emotionally of course).

It is a small additional subtle pressure. It's like putting a lot of pressure on your partner when he is reversing into a parking space. For the restaurant it's the same thing, but more subtle. As I say, this is not an obligation. It may be hard to think about it at the right time.

Your interlocutor is now tied to his chair, but he does not know it yet.

You will make a direct attack, you can use the relocation of the source(to make him believe that your are not behind what you say).

But!

Do not ask questions! You must claim the things. Do not say: "are you unfaithful?".

Of course you will observe reactions, but here, it is not just about collecting information, but to push your interlocutor to tell the truth. So do not ask questions, because when you do that he could think that you do not know the truth.

For example, you can say: "I know you're going to lie to me, but I know .... I know everything, you are deceiving me!." And remember the power of the silence.

Now the lamp in the face... Your spouse will at this moment suffer a huge pressure. His limbic brain will react faster than he wants and this provokes reactions. he'll suddenly realize how much he is stuck. He will make all sorts of gestures defence, self-massage, and will respond with the different sentences previously seen in this book, in brief, all the reactions that we talked about.

Besides the feeling of being trapped and unable to escape, you claim that it is just a waste of time to lie to you because you know the truth (even if it is not the case)! You must never allow him to have other option. Remember! The objectives are to observe the reactions, to notice the signs of lies and to collapse under pressure. And what pressure!

Come on, it's not over, if after all signs of lies you've spotted your interlocutor persist in his lie, then use the following technique. You can create a big hole in the wall with a sentence like this: "well, actually I thought a lot about it, you know what I feel for you, and I think I can accept it."

This type of sentence can be magical, because you let your prey (sorry, your spouse) believe that it does not matter, that you forgive him. He surely thinks that you give him a way out which allow him to break out of this unbearable pressure.

He will probably think something like that: "What? She said that it was not serious? Wow! That's good, I'll be able to get rid of this pressure, all right, I admit it ".

The most important points of this technique and all the elements that make up it, are the pressure, the stress and emotion, the limbic response and the physical reaction. If you always consider this common denominators, if you have to properly prepare the ground fresh in your mind, then you will be able to build and develop your own methods.

This chapter is now finished, you learned tactical, strategic and offensive techniques. If observation and information gathering (in a stealth way)   are good things it could be possible in some situations that you are forced to attack.

Now you have more weapons in your arsenal.

We will attack the next chapter it contains the latest works about which I worked on these last few months in my laboratory. These techniques were tested and checked on everyone around me with success. I leave you to discover ...

Chapter 7

ADVANCED TECHNIQUES
-
RESEARCH & DEVELOPMENT

In this chapter, we will discuss about the eyes direction in a very specific case. Then we will study with an advanced technique, eyes direction when someone speak and the link between eyes and the value of the speech. We'll also talk about what I called micro-shifts and conclude this chapter by the technique of time distortion and its counter-attack.

Do you remember the chapter about eyes direction which depends on whether someone is searching in his memory for information or he is inventing something.

There is an important element to be taken into account, the ratio time / complexity of the information that you need remember. let' s take an example ,you hold a card game out to me, ask me to choose a random card and to memorize it.

I saved the Jack of spades, then you show me the cards one by one, while asking me if this is the card I have in memory. This can also be a good practice for detecting reactions (other than the eyes), to do with your friends.

In fact I just memorized the card which is not a very complex information to memorize, then I do not need to direct my eyes to the left to search information in my memory. So I can stare at you and lie to you. However, if two weeks later you ask me the question: "What was your card?", maybe I will not remember it , or at least I do not remember if it was a spade or a club, so I will definitely look toward the left to search it in my memories.
Therefore, the ratio time / complexity of the information must be taken into account. In fact, the eyes direction is a technique that absolutely must be combined with others because of its possible variants, like being left-or right-handed, for example.

People often ask me if someone who train to lie can look in the eyes while he lies. This is difficult to do, but it is still possible. it could be done only for answers which have been created and learned by heart before the conversation. At the last question that will be calling on the memory of the liar, the eyes direction will become normal.

With practice, you can shorten the time the eyes movement takes. But that involves that you exercise a conscious control over this reflex, a move that will be quickly harm by the limbic brain which foils your attempt, now know how to provoke limbic reactions!

Among the questions that people asked me too, there is a recurrent one, don't you think that someone who lies will search your approval, so he will stare at you. Most of the time people who lie have their eyes down because they are afraid that through his eyes you can read the truth.

Then, as soon as he stops to speak (to lie) he has no reason to be afraid, so he can look you straight in the eye to make sure that you believed him. In the paragraph of speech we will see quickly an example about the evasive glances.

You must take all these subtleties into account.

We'll see the example of someone who trains to lie and who could use a particular technique to try to hide or sow doubts in your mind by the movement of his eyes. someone who tries to hide his eyes movement may try to do this: imagine that I am in front of you, I have to use my memory then my eyes will move logically to the left. A second later I realize and I try to hide this movement so I turn my head in the same direction than my eyes ! ".

When I do that, my head turns to the left so my eyes and my head will be in the same direction which will allow me to think in peace. My interlocutor will wonder, if I'm thinking or if I invent something or make a call to my memory .

It's the only time that I met someone who used this technique, it was with the intention to quickly hide the direction of his eyes. This is rare but you could see it one day.

The following two concepts we going to look at now are about the eyes, just like people who make a speech on the television.

The only disadvantage of this medium is the frequent changes of camera angles that make us miss most of the limbic reactions. The cameras are pointed too long to the person who asked the question rather than go immediately to the interviewee.
But in the following example, it was rather easy to detect lie.

As you know, the rule is that someone who lies you glances away. He is afraid that you can see his lie through his eyes or maybe he is ashamed. It's a classic reaction.

The person who lies but may be ashamed, never looks you straight in the eye. But there is another scenario linked to people who practice lying and who have no sense of guilt.

These people look you straight in the eye all the time they speak to you, then, when they start to lie, just at this moment, their glance down.
When they stop to lie, they stare at you again, or at the objective. From now on, you will take a critical look at the speeches.

Recently, in a major ecological disaster in the United States, an official said, while looking straight in the eye of reporters and cameras present, that all means were employed to resolve promptly the problem.

This official did not take his eyes off his audience for a second during his speech, **except** when he said " there is no oil leak and if there is one it will have no effect on the environment".

Then he carried on his speech his eyes fixed on his interlocutors. If you take his speech in its entirety (without mentioning limbic reactions or types of responses), and if you listen the television without watching it, you will think that he is sincere and that the problem will be resolved quickly and without damage. Absolutely not !
First I did not question the fact that all means were made to

resolve the problem, but when he lowered his eyes, I understand that his words did not the reflect of his thoughts (clearly he lied). Moreover, making the connection between this gesture and the words: "there are no leaks and if there is one it will have no impact on the environment" it was obvious that he hided something. A few days later the facts confirmed my detection.

As in this example, during a speech, you must pay attention to **what your interlocutor says and his eyes direction** or movements.

Last evening, as I watched a programme on television, I was surprised to see this man, a so-called expert speaking about a subject that he was supposed mastering, he never stopped to read his notes. A real expert doesn't need notes, he is able to speak about what he really master, so I wondered if I had missed a great percentage of lies.

Indeed, why it could not be possible to use a sheet of paper to cover up our lie? Not to hide our face with it, but imagine the following scenario. Mr. X makes his speech in a convincing manner and looks his interlocutors straight in the eye. Then, when he starts to lie he lowers his gaze (like the example above) except that it seems he just reads his notes! I tell you, this technique is widely used ...

How to detect if it is a lie? Play as if there was no sheet of paper and listen carefully to the words related to movement of the eyes. Is this an important answer to a important question ? Pay attention to the following point: what it could be consequences if he had answered differently?

For example: imagine the case of the previous ecological disaster. If the communications consultant gave the opposite answer: "yes there is a large oil spill and environmental consequences will be significant." . It is a very important thing to hide !

We must make the link between the reaction you've detected and the words (their importance) you heard.

The techniques of compression and distortion of time.

Some people gifted in the art of lying are able to use what I call the compression of time. How does it specifically work ? In fact it is very simple and the results are very effective so it becomes very difficult to detect lies.
Time compression is the technique of taking a real event and to use it as a lie.
Let's consider this example: you have doubts about the faithfulness of your partner. You ask her the following question: "So, how was your evening?" And she gives you a detailed answer, with some emotions, feelings and opinions of those present at this evening (like the latest example of responses we discussed in the paragraph on "response with variable geometry).

This response which moreover is supported by open gestures, direct gaze, calls to her memory, in short, you can not detect any signs of lies. But she actually having an affair with another man, and this evening she spent her time with him. But what happened ? Have you lost your legendary power ? No. Has she lied ? Either.
This is the time compression effect. Experienced liars will divide the evening into two parts. The first part of the evening, she had a drink with her friends and she took care to note and memorize trivia, words exchanged, all that could detail the scene.
In fact it is not very difficult to memorize this evening because she really lived all this details. She even takes care to keep some details aside for the next time. Then, when you will ask the question, you'll get a sincere response. She will tell you the first part of the evening but omitted the second one which corresponds to her affair.

It's child's play, isn't it?

The distortion of time is a variant of this technique because the professional liar calls old memories, such as when she had a drink in the last month with her friends but you didn't know about it.
So she can use these elements keep her cards close to her chest.

Another example: You know that your spouse has a dinner tonight but you have doubts about who will be with her, you think that one of her colleagues who runs after her could be present.

The experienced liar who wants to be as credible as possible, may organize a lunch with one of her colleagues, and record all the details, so In this specific evening (with his lover) she will tell you her lunch, she will do it with conviction because it is really what happened.

How to detect the lies with such effective techniques ?

The method of the restaurant (the psychological trap) that simulates the pressure of a police questioning (you saw the effects in the previous chapter) is the most effective. The attacks by allusions, especially the technique of the nightmare can have a powerful effect on your interlocutor.

In fact, all techniques which don't take the liar talking into account. But if you persist in looking for signs in her history, even with the proper techniques you will get nothing because this story is real.

Of course, I suggest you to look for signs in her history, after all, you do not know if she is lying.
After a while, if you find nothing, using a technique that does not take her history into account.

Indeed, with the direct attack, you will surprise your partner, because she will say: "Oh damn! I strained myself for nothing, he thinks I have an affair with someone! what am I going to answer him? ".

You may well also ask: "and then what did you do in the second part of the evening? "That could eventually cause this effect !

The micro-gap.

The concept of micro-gap, is when someone tries to feign anger, tries to support it with a gesture. It's kind of desynchronization.

An angry person will bang his fist on the table and express his anger simultaneously. Someone who will try to convince you of his angry will first speak (more or less convincingly) and then bang his fist on the table. This therefore means that he is not so angry that he want to make you think.

Have you ever heard someone on TV speaking but, despite the vehemence of his words and his wish to convince you that he is sincere you feel that something is wrong. Even if he smiles, his gesture to support his claim, you could not believe what he says.

That's what I call micro-gap. This is a subtle and very slight difference between what someone says and his gestures. To realise of it, try to lie. But not just a little, ask someone you know to observe you and inform him that the story you tell is true. Then, create and tell him a false story. Invent all the details but try to support your false words with gestures and looked him straight in the eye.

You can do it alone with a mirror, and if you do not have a mirror, try to imagine the scene. is it more difficult than you thought ?

There are chances that your gesture are not really synchronized with your words. Experienced liars train to make wide gestures while they speak. They may come close to perfection but there will always be a small gap which will give you the feeling that something is wrong. You can find this case of micro-gap when someone hide his emotions not necessarily in order to lie. He does not want to reveal anything to the others and give the impression of being insensitive, or that they feel no emotions. So to hide this feeling, he will consciously make gestures to accompany their words but you will feel this gap.

This is because unconsciously, you perceive a micro-lag !
To counter these micro-gap, you will use techniques that have no link with body language as we have studied in a previous chapter.

In fact limbic reactions work perfectly because these gaps are only about the gestures and speeches.

This chapter is now finished and we will start the next chapter. It will give you a training method to become more effective in your lie detection quest.

Chapter 8

MENTAL TRAINING TECHNIQUES

Every day, it is an easy thing to observe people around you during conversations, in order to practice to detect any lies, take your time and have fun. Even if you cannot clearly identify the limbic responses, it does not matter you have all the time in the world.

Later in the day, if you realize that you missed a gesture or movements «drat it! In retrospect he had a reaction when I told him this or that", well it does not matter, the next time you will surely think about it.

Now, imagine that you are more effective, you have already intercepted signals lies in your contacts. Nevertheless, this time when you were with this particular person you have been disturbed so much so, that you forget to look for signs of lies. Maybe it was a difficult one emotionally, maybe your spouse was your interlocutor, about whom you are suspicious or even your boss, your colleague on who you have some resentment.

Your emotion is so stronger that it has upset your lucidity. You no longer think to pay attention to signals, or even to be able to think at all. Then when the hurricane went, you had recovered your faculties. Without going to talk about difficult situations, when we observe two people talking, it is very easy to take time to observe them.

But, when we are implicated in the conversation, sometimes you can be confuse and you forget to identify the signals.

These disorders were related to feelings so to the emotions and our limbic brain begins to react and brings about a "power cut" in your conscious brain (the neocortex).

When this "mental break" ends, you pick up your minds.

Thanks to the mental techniques that I developed from my experience over twenty years in the practice of martial arts, I will give you some keys to develop the following abilities.

- Learn and assimilate as fast as possible the techniques of this book, and any other skills (intellectual, athletic or manual).
- Develop strong power of concentration that will allow you to

stay focused on detecting lies and does not leave you disturbed by external factors.
- And finally, develop a degree of self-control sufficiently developed to cope with difficult situations.

It is a big jump between the words "assimilate" and "learn" the techniques to detect lies. Learn things depend largely on you but there is still a way to accelerate learning.

We will focus on assimilation or rather, on what I call the digestion of information, in this way they become reflexes. Learned information is one thing, but to become an automatic reflex is another. We will broach this point so that all the information in this book becomes reflexes as expeditiously as possible.

In this chapter, when I talk about reflexes, it is not limbic reflexes (in fact the term "reflex" inaccurate, it would be more appropriate to say limbic "reactions", which are faster than reflexes).
Indeed, you may have the highest mastery of yourself, if a car suddenly runs over you when you cross the road, your limbic system will bypass all your reflexes "learned" and make you react to this situation.

The limbic system is linked to the survival instinct of the human being and it has a much faster system than all the reflexes that you could build in your memory.

Besides, we have to admit that it is a stroke of luck!
We will start by learning the information. Did you find it easier to learn something when that thing is nice? When you were at school, did you come up against subjects which set you really problems? And so, didn't you have some difficulties to memorize and to learn these subjects? How is it possible that you memorize some things better than others?

This is because when you store information you associate with them more or less strong emotions.

As you know, the limbic system is the seat of emotions and the system which manages memory is in this place too. And what's more it seems that the memorization process is an emotional one.
It is not surprising that when you feel pleasure to do or learn something you get there more easily! I'm sure that you easily recall these pleasant moments spent on holiday, the intense moments of your life. Because in that case you were in a very emotional moment and these experiences were imprinted easily and strongly on your memory.

If you read this book, it is because you are motivated, because you want to learn, and this is an emotion so you quickly learn the information, I bet you that if I tell you to stop reading this book and give you a maths book instead it could be hard to do!

The reverse is true, I mean for bad experiences or when harsh hardship hurts you, and then you felt a very strong emotion which will be set in stone for the rest of your life.

As the memorization of information is an emotional process, the advertising specialists use that knowledge to sell you their products. Indeed, if you pay attention, good advertising should put you in a state, or generate an emotion in you by different way one of them is the humor.

Once you're laughing, you are in a state of joy (emotion), and it is exactly when the product appears! Your brain then stores more deeply the information without your noticing anything.

Another method of advertising is to display things to touch your sensitivity such as animals (baby animals are better) or children, in short, all sensitive cases. That brings you joy, gives you great pleasure and again generates well-being, then the product will be present to you. And of course you will store more deeply the information.

Watch advertisement on television and you'll see …

Why not use this technique to better learn the information in this book, or any other book, or to learn anything faster?

I've practised this technique to learn for many years, it is very simple, so simple that one might wonder if it really works.
But in fact, knowing now the mechanism of memory you'll have no trouble to create your own technique yourself! Even if you are motivated to learn, using this technique you will learn even faster. What is the secret?

For me it's the music ... It could seem stupid, but when I need to learn something very quickly I put the headphones on my ears and listen to music. Of course the music I love, which gets me in a strong emotional state and I read…

I think you understood, I memorize the information more deeply because I'm motivated by this strong emotional state.

Of course, to more emphasize this effect, you can think of all the profits, the joy you will have when you reach your goals, but this will be the subject of the following technique: the visualization and whose this aim is to help you to assimilate and to transform information into reflexes.

You can create your own technique as long as you get yourself in a good emotional state. This may be the relaxation for example, you're lying on your sofa, listening soft music and so you enjoy this moment ... So you have emotions and you will memorize more easily, more quickly and for ever the information you want to learn.

Another example, it could be a walk in the woods, on the beach or somewhere you really like, do something you like, that gives you emotion while you learn.

Personally, I love the art of listening to music with headphones on my ears. You must be stirred when listen your music, it must generates the most emotion in yourself ...

And you, what is your technique ?

Learning is one thing, take in information is another. How to speed up the process? By visualization! But before we talk about it, I suggest you to dissect the concept of reflex. How to build a reflex? Let's look more closely at the action in slow motion!
Take the example of boxing: to give a punch, and to maximize the power of this movement, the coach of boxing will make you execute the movement slowly.

You will dissect the gesture, until you understand the movement, then you will repeat it and repeat it slowly until you will achieve perfection.

You will make the movement in space, then you will do it on a punching bag, and you will repeat the movement again and again. After a number of training hours this gesture will become gradually a reflex, you will not need to dissect carefully the action to execute, you will do it automatically.
During all those hours of training, you will focus on the movement, you will look in the mirror trying to execute this movement. your brain will remember this action and this movement will become a conditioned reflex.

How to speed up this process? I'm sure you've already done, and probably without even realizing it.If you're a fan of boxing (of course, you can adapt it to your passion), the training session is not sufficient, and when you get home, you can not stop to think about it, you will keep turning over this training session, in short, you'll visualize all these repetitions of gestures. Well, believe it or not, but doing this exercise, will speed up the impregnation, it is the same thing than to participate in a second boxing training ! (Not for the physical tiredness but for memorizing the gesture).

As this gesture is in your brain (you learned it and memorized it) so let's work our brains (to equate the gesture).

Believe me I used visualization for years (and even before without know it) and I can assure you that I am able to assimilate much faster any skill or technique than anyone who does not use the visualization .

This technique is used in relaxation therapy and by some top athletes. For example, you may have seen the skiers, who imagine mentally the race they will do before a competition, or even, the Formula 1 drivers who mentally view all corners of the circuit on which they will to race.

They train their brains to assimilate quickly the circuit in order to be more effective on the day of the competition. Arnold Schwarzenegger himself used this technique when he was at his highest level in body-building and he's something of a trail-blazer in the visualization method.

How do I proceed to digest a complex technique? I put my walk-man on the ears and I visualize myself trying to execute this complex technique, I repeat in my head again and again (and again).

I imagine the scene as if it was real, so I have the impression of being really in training, I feel the same joy of being able to properly execute the movement against my opponent!

I can also imagine the congratulations of my coach. By doing this, I feel emotions, so I intensify the recording of this gesture in my brain.

If you're really serious, the next time you train, you will have great opportunities to perform this movement almost automatically before the astonished gaze of your team member!
What will they think about you? Maybe that you have talent for it, so it's normal that you progress faster. We know that it is not the

truth, but you, unlike the others, you use your brain as an additional tool for training.

That is why there is a difference between someone good, someone very good and a champion.

The secret to an effective visualization is divided into two parts: Once you've learned something (and I mean just learned), **that thing is in your brain** and when you practice (a real or mental practice), you must understand that **your brain can not make difference**.

The second part of this secret lies in the fact that the emotions you feel when you make your mental visualization. Remember, emotions are linked to the limbic brain, you know that at this place where your memory is managed and don't forget that memorization is an emotional process!

If you still doubt, just think about all your memories saved because of or thanks to the emotions you had during the events.

In concrete terms, what use will the mental visualization be, and what is the link with lies detection? The purpose of this chapter is to bring you a tool to deal with difficult situations, which put you through the mill. Mental visualization will help you to prepare yourself for a difficult situation in which you have to be at the top to sort the truth out from the lies.

If you apply these techniques and practice seriously you will turn all these information into reflexes and you'll be ready at the right. Maybe not a hundred per cent, but more over than if you decide to do nothing and stay paralyzed by the emotions.
Mental visualization could help you to quickly assimilate the contents of this book and further this will help you to prepare for the behavior you will have in response to this situation.

For example, instead of learning to give a punch you will learn to stay calm, to control your emotions during the "confrontation"

particularly if usually you find it 's too hard to do it.
How?
By use again the principle of the boxing exercise of which I talked about earlier. A little later we will work with a specific example but before we'll talk about mental concentration.

What is the uses of concentration? As I said in the introduction, you can be disturbed by an external event which can make you miss the limbic reaction of your interlocutor.

Or, simply the fact that you can be under the contact what I call "looking straight in the eye" and its fascinating power which has disturbed you.

Of course, you can practice mental visualization to overcome this problem, but I'll just give you some exercises to do if you have a problem of concentration.

The aim of this practice is for you to manage to stay focused on something without diverting your attention not once.

Exercise 1:
Rather difficult, you may not be able to do this exercise until the end but try to do it as long as possible.
Sit down somewhere and put before you an analog clock (if possible without the second hand), or an alarm clock (a digital watch should be very good).
Your mission, if you accept it, is to fix the clock for an hour without looking away or thinking about other thing than the clock, you just need to focus on the hands of the clock without thinking of something else.

If you practice this exercise regularly, I can assure you that you'll have a so powerful glance that you could melt an object just by looking it !

Seriously, you'll be able to observe your partner while staying focused on your goal, which is to detect the lies!

Now a little more difficult exercise, you will do again the same exercise but this time you'll fix something less attractive than a clock. For example, push a thumbtack in the middle of the wall on your living room, grab a chair, sit down and fix the thumbtack for an hour without looking away, and, staying concentrate... It is more difficult, is not it? Fix yourself a time limit as 10 minutes before to begin the exercise, this should be enough.

If you catch yourself distracting your eyes or if you realize that your mind is elsewhere, no problem, concentrate again on the clock or the thumbtack and try to keep as long as possible.

Do this exercise regularly and you'll be surprised how your concentration will be developed.

This exercise will give you an added advantage, you can increase your concentration during your visualization sessions and thus increase its effect.

It must be charity week! Here is one more which will train you to develop your mental visualization. While it is easy to imagine a situation that we like (as the example of boxing training) it is rather more difficult to concentrate on a visual image which does no of interest you.

Take yourself comfortable on a chair, a sofa, or a bench, and focus on a mental image. Imagine a mental clock that you previously set in your living room for real and try to stay focused on this mental image as long as possible.

Try to imagine this clock as accurately as possible and stay focused on it! Come on, you can try to view another object, I give you permission .... You can visualize a car, a person, or anything you want. For example you can choose a picture and then close your eyes and try to reproduce this picture mentally and try to stay focused over ten minutes.

These exercises have a beneficial effect because they can develop a so great strength of concentration than you can concentrate all your attention in one place and think more effectively to a problem.

You can relentlessly search to resolve your problem without your attention being disturbed by external factors or by yourself (your emotions related to this particular problem)
It's the purpose of the following examples.

You've got to quickly learn more information, you learned to faster assimilate this information, to turn it into reflexes, you learned to develop your concentration, and now you're ready for the final training that will prepare you to brave difficult situations, or simply improve your effectiveness in everyday life.

The advantage of these exercises and these techniques of mental training is that you can adapt them to every domain, competences, manual skills, sports performance, self-control and so on . we will broach a specific scenario, rather complex, but that will give you the opportunity to easily adapt it to the simpler cases.

Scenario:
You're Mrs. Y, you're married for several years but unfortunately you suspect your husband of being unfaithful. You are not sure and you even think that it is not the first time. You think that you might be divorced but you have not yet seriously considered it.
In the immediate future, your first idea is to try to detect lies in what your husband tells you. But there is a big problem, your husband becomes aggressive, so it's very difficult to ask him questions when you try to broach the subject with him.

You're scared or you are angry, but these emotions paralyze you totally even to the point that you finally think that it is better to give up to know the truth. For example, when you try to ask him questions more or less directly (to avoid to draw his attention to the subject) he aggressively replies, although you suspect him to hide something you're afraid about his reaction to such an extent that you forget to detect signs of lies.

How to adapt the techniques of this chapter to this situation? How to try to stay lucid despite these emotional tensions?

The first question to ask yourself is: what I exactly want to do? Example: do you want to stay calm when you ask the fateful question and identify all the signs that reveal his lies, and more difficult, to confound him about his lies and finally take a decision?

Once you know exactly what you want, you must work on these points. To stay lucid, at least to a sufficient level, you must work your concentration, with the previous exercise, as strange as that they could be seem, so you have just to stay focused on one thing as long as you can.
This also could help you to stand back from all the disturbing elements inherent to this point and so you will remain lucid. Then add the exercises of mental visualization, make yourself comfortable and practice mentally in order to cope with this specific situation, don't lose sight of the goal you want to achieve. In order to stay lucid must practice it in your mind! Visualize yourself in the face of your husband who usually makes you lose your head.

But now the opposite will happen, visualize exactly the aim you want to achieve and remain lucid, imagine yourself remaining unmoved by what he will say, you are completely lucid and you can detect all lies one after the other. Imagine that you are yourself ... impressed!

Do you understand what I mean? Feel through this mental exercise how you are so happy to have got what you want, in short, fell these emotions!

Thus you will fix it firmly and quickly in your mind this new reflex which will replace the old one. The more you do this exercise with emotions the faster this reflex will be developed, and the day of the confrontation you'll be much more lucid than you would have never believed....

The fatal day, the most important question to ask yourself is: what exactly do I want to do? (As I usually say, in life you can choose any direction, but until you know where you go it is important to know where you are right now). What will you tell him? What are the specific points I will deal with him during the confrontation?

Once you've answered these questions you can, like the Formula one driver who mentally visualized the circuit on which it is running, prepare yourself to this confrontation.
Visualize yourself, quiet strength, calm and indifferent to his reactions, imagine you laying down your questions and discovering all his lies, imagine his violent reactions having no impact on you.

Go onto asking questions with emotions, testing out the joy to succeed, imagine the reaction of your friends when you tell them how you solved the problem, in short, practice yourself mentally!

The aim of this chapter and the last example is to give you some techniques which will allow you to be more effective in lies detection. According the situations, it may not be obvious for everyone to stay enough lucid to really detect them.

You can adapt the last example to your own situation. Are you just a little distracted? Shy? Are you afraid to stare at your audience? Are you afraid about your next interview?

Do you think that you could not detect lies very quickly? Do you want to acquire a great ability that will allow you to detect any reaction of lies without even to concentrate on it (like a conditioned reflex)?
Now you know what you have to do, it occurred in your mind, then you have to define exactly what you want, to practice mental visualization and you will surprised by the quickness of the results!

CONCLUSION

Here is the end of this little book of lie detection. I hope that you liked it and that it give you the desire you to become a lies detector!

More seriously, the modest aim of this little book is first to give you tools and techniques which will help you to develop and to improve your vigilance.

And if that is the case now, so I'm happy.

Don't forget :

- to practice, the exercises and techniques are simple, so you stand a good chance of succeeding.
- to take into account that even you discover a (single) lie from your interlocutor you can't immediately say that he is a liar!

As I suggested earlier in this book, create a list in your mind and write down all your clues!

I wish you a good practice and most importantly thing, have fun!

Sincerely,

Philippe Kaizen

Here is below, my two other books about lie detection:

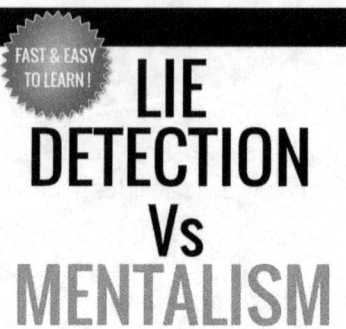

FAST & EASY TO LEARN!

LIE DETECTION Vs MENTALISM

Pragmatic strategies for detecting lies and enhancing your skills.

PHILIPPE KAIZEN

PHILIPPE KAIZEN

LIE DETECTION

AND EYE MOVEMENTS

How to spot liars with this in-depth analysis of eye movement

PHILIPPE KAIZEN

www.ingramcontent.com/pod-product-compliance
Lightning Source LLC
Chambersburg PA
CBHW06201228052б
45787CB00005B/2080